BEING JOSHUA

— Being Believers —

BEING JOSHUA

Essential Elements of the Christian Walk

Rev. Archie Murray

BEING JOSHUA
Copyright © 2021 by Rev. Archie Murray

All rights reserved. Neither this publication nor any part of this publication may be reproduced or transmitted in any form or by any means, electronic or mechanical, including photocopying, recording or any information storage and retrieval system, without permission in writing from the author.

Unless otherwise indicated, all scripture quotations are taken from the New King James Version®. Copyright © 1982 by Thomas Nelson. Used by permission. All rights reserved. Scripture quotations marked ESV are taken from The Holy Bible, English Standard Version, Copyright © 2001 by Crossway, a publishing ministry of Good News Publishers. Used by permission. All rights reserved. Scripture quotations marked KJV are taken from the Holy Bible, King James Version, which is in the public domain. Scripture quotations marked NIV are taken from The Holy Bible, New International Version® NIV® Copyright © 1973 1978 1984 2011 by Biblica, Inc. TM Used by permission. All rights reserved worldwide. Scripture marked NLT are taken from the Holy Bible, New Living Translation, Copyright © 1996, 2004, 2007 by Tyndale House Foundation. Used by permission of Tyndale House Publishers, Inc., Carol Stream, Illinois 60188. All rights reserved.

Print ISBN: 978-1-4866-2213-9
eBook ISBN: 978-1-4866-2214-6

Word Alive Press
119 De Baets Street, Winnipeg, MB R2J 3R9
www.wordalivepress.ca

Cataloguing in Publication may be obtained through Library and Archives Canada

The Being Believers series is dedicated to my brother
Robert F. Murray

Robert led me to Jesus Christ and won me for Him when we were both teenagers. He has been a lifetime example for me, as my brother John has also been, who since early childhood made me proud.

—Rev. Archie Murray, BD, DipMin, DPT

CONTENTS

Acknowledgements … xiii
Introduction … xv

SECTION I: BORN FOR A PURPOSE

1. Being Joshua … 3
2. Being Born … 5
3. Being Aware … 7
4. Being Given Hope … 9

SECTION II: EARLY LIFE AND LEARNING

5. Being Something When You Are Nothing … 13
6. Being Aware of God … 15
7. Faith + Pain = Preparation … 17
8. Being a Functioning Society of Slaves … 19

SECTION III: MOSES AND THE EXODUS

9. Deserts Being Springboards … 25
10. The Gospel in Exodus … 29
11. Being Re-Defined … 33
12. Problems Being Propellants … 35
13. Listening with Faith … 37

SECTION IV: BEING A WANDERER

14. Being in the Desert … 43
15. Amalek Repulsed … 45
16. Being in Prayer … 47
17. Being Written Down … 49
18. Being Ready to Fight … 51

SECTION V: MOUNTAINS AND MEN

19. Being Alone   57
20. What Kind of Noise Are We Making?   59
21. Being Unable to Stand   63
22. Being a Choice Man   65

SECTION VI: INAUGURATION

23. People Being Fickle   71
24. Being Inaugurated   73
25. Being Encouraged   77
26. Being Watched   79
27. Being Moses's Successor   81

SECTION VII: THEREFORE ARISE AFTER MOSES

28. After the Death of Moses   85
29. Therefore Arise   89
30. Being More than Yourself   91

SECTION VIII: COMPELLING AND CONTROLLED

31. Joshua's Faith   95
32. Faith Large, but Limited   97
33. Faith Has Enemies   99
34. Faith with Heart and Obedience   101

SECTION IX: JOSHUA STEPS UP

35. The Big Picture   105
36. The Small Detail   107
37. Unity in Mutual Exhortation   109

SECTION X: THE CITY, THE INHABITANT, THE SPIES

38. Introduction to Jericho   113
39. Being the Home of Rahab   115
40. Being Hidden   117

41.	Rahab and the King	119
42.	A Virtuous Woman	121
43.	Being Breached	123
44.	Time to Repent	125
45.	Being Talked About	127
46.	Rahab's Profession of Faith	129
47.	A Simple Red Cord	131

SECTION XI: THE CITY

48.	The Rise of Cities	137
49.	The City (Part 1)	139
50.	The City (Part 2)	141
51.	A Generation of Degradation	143
52.	God Being Angry	145

SECTION XII: THE JORDAN CROSSING

53.	Preparation for Punishment	149
54.	Keep Your Distance	151
55.	You Have Not Passed This Way Before	153
56.	This Jordan	155
57.	Sanctification	157
58.	Being Exalted	161
59.	Being Able to Stand in Your Jordan	163

SECTION XIII: OBEDIENCE, THE CEREMONY OF A BELIEVING HEART

60.	Come Here and Hear	167
61.	Forty Years to Take a Few Steps	169
62.	Take a Stand on the Problem	171
63.	God Near at Hand and God Afar Off	173
64.	Memorial Stones	175
65.	Stones That Speak	177
66.	Being the Teacher	181

SECTION XIV: IS GOD FOR US OR AGAINST US?

67. Ceremony Before Service — 185
68. The Commander of the Armies of the Lord — 189
69. Are You for Us or against Us? — 193
70. Christ in All the Scriptures — 195

SECTION XV: UNDERSTANDING DEVOTED TO DESTRUCTION

71. Jericho, an Assessment — 201
72. Jericho… SHUT UP! — 203
73. The Art of War — 205
74. Understanding Devotion — 207
75. Saved Amidst Destruction — 209
76. Theological History — 213
77. Being the Only Good Thing in Jericho — 215
78. God Reveals Himself to Us — 217

SECTION XVI: FOUR WORDS FOR "PRESENCE"

79. Being Famous — 221
80. Being a Trespasser — 223
81. God Being Angry — 225
82. Presence Being Four Words — 227
83. We are Never Alone — 231
84. Being Just a Little Town — 233
85. Being Quiet Before Judgement — 235
86. God Being against Us — 237

SECTION XVII: THE PROBLEM IS AMONG OUR OWN 'STUFF'

87. God No Longer with Us — 241
88. Worship Being Examined — 243
89. The Problem is among Our Own 'Stuff' — 245
90. Being Gentle with the Guilty — 249
91. The Valley of Trouble — 251

SECTION XVIII: BEING BACK TO WHERE YOU STARTED

92. God is Gentle with Joshua — 255
93. Doing Things Right — 257
94. Joshua Renews the Covenant — 259

SECTION XIX: BEING DECEIVED

95. The Deception of Gibeon — 265
96. Leaders Being Fooled — 269
97. Faith is Instant — 273
98. Leaders Must Be Thorough — 275
99. The Battle is Not the End of the Event — 277

SECTION XX: PROMISE BEING FULFILLED

100. Of the Southland — 283
101. The Northern Conquest — 285
102. Timing — 287
103. Leave Nothing Undone — 289
104. Being Generous — 291
105. Six Years of Problems into One Short Sentence — 293
106. Prepare for Old Age — 295
107. Borders Are Essential — 297
108. Do Not Despise Small Things — 299
109. Inability and Refusal — 301
110. Are You Who You Think You Are? — 303

SECTION XXI: ENTER IN!

111. The Saddest Verse in Joshua — 307
112. Being Negligent — 309
113. Being Surveyors — 311
114. Joshua's Inheritance — 313
115. The Cities of Refuge — 315
116. The Promise Fulfilled — 317

SECTION XXII: END TIMES BEING A MODERN PROBLEM

117.	The Two-and-a-Half Tribes	321
118.	A Gossip is among Us!	325
119.	The Lord is among Us	329

SECTION XXIII: CHOOSE TODAY

120.	Joshua's Farewell Address	333
121.	The Word of God Being Front and Centre	335

SECTION XXIV: LAST WORDS

122.	Last Words Being Impressive	341
123.	Preach It, Brother!	343
124.	The Death of Joshua and Eleazar	347

Conclusion	349
About the Author	351

ACKNOWLEDGEMENTS

As always, my greatest support comes from my wife Helen, who unceasingly encourages me to write. To Michael and Martha for their unwavering practical and prayerful partnership in this series of books. My joyful thanks to Emmett, Brooklyn and Victoria, my grandchildren who bring a deep worthwhile purpose into my life and regularly check in to make sure I am working! Jonathan, Rosslyn, and Allison all have made the work of writing easier by their faithful and inspiring encouragement. Also, to many others for their emails, calls, and comments that assure me God has touched their lives by these humble books. Finally, to my very good friends who kept me sane through all the work… HyeJung, SangDon, Jong-Hyung, and HyoJin on whose computer I wrote this particular book. Those known and unknown to me who pray for me should know that I have felt their help and stayed the course—their reward is in heaven. The secret things belong to the Lord.

INTRODUCTION

This is the third book in the series *Being Believers*. The two previous books, *Being Joseph* and *Being Ruth*, dealt mainly with domestic situations. This book is about the man, Joshua. He is a warrior statesman. We will draw lessons from the Bible and the Book of Joshua without straying too far from the man himself. The lessons, challenges, and blessings demonstrated in his life are pertinent for every believer.

The book is both pastoral and practical. It is relevant to the daily life of all believers. We must aspire to godly character and poise, spirituality, learning, and experience. Like Joshua, we must go up and possess the land.

Joshua spans an incredible time in the history of Israel. Born in Egyptian slavery, Joshua experienced the Exodus with Moses, crossed the Red Sea, and was on Sinai when Moses received the Ten Commandments. Joshua wandered the wilderness and then led the conquest and settling of Canaan, the Promised Land. His was an amazing time, an amazing life. Yours can be too.

Most readers are unlikely to be warriors and statesmen. But the average believer must change. We must recognize ourselves as different in God's eyes, then live like we believed this truth. If you naturally lean towards fighting, arguing, and denouncing everything... you aren't what I am advocating. You need to learn more peaceful ways—God's warfare isn't a justification for rage.

Sir Walter Scott, in his novel *Waverley*, illustrates that going to court to ruin your enemy is just the same as the rage of the ancient who burned his enemy's castle to the ground then hit him on the head as he tried to escape the conflagration![1] Rage isn't the biblical concept of 'righteous indignation.' Rage isn't part of the Christian's armoury. We don't need courts or the weapons of modern warfare. We have the word of God and prayer, as Paul says, "*...and the Sword of the Spirit, which is the word of God; praying always...*" (Ephesians 6: 17–18).

So, settle down, this book is for ordinary believers who need to awaken to their unique role as ambassadors for Christ and His cause. God determined that we would win the world primarily with words, His words, harmonized with daily, practical godliness: a powerful force, like the irresistible movement of the ocean's tides. The only part of my enemy that may experience 'smiting' will be his conscience. A well-presented Biblical case from the feeblest believer can evoke a good response, where a bully with a club will fail.

Believers will find a particular affinity with Joshua because he walked with God in every situation. While being a great warrior, Joshua still comes across as an endearing character.

I am writing this book because there is a need for believers to be "very courageous," and to grasp again that "the Lord Our God is with us!" For a century, the church has been silenced and bullied without cause. Believers today need to speak up again, be strong, and declare the good news of the gospel of Jesus Christ.

This isn't a book on evangelism as such. It is a book about being a man of God. Not a book about *speaking* but about *being* something, about listening and living for God. Such a life will produce people who speak at every level of the art.

It is time our present-day 'Jerichos' were "*shut up* and *closed down!*" This can be achieved by gentle, humble, believing men of God. The book isn't a call to organize anything or a precursor to campaign for anything novel or new. It is a genuine call to radical, daily faith and practice. Joshua learned God's ways. He went on to achieve great things. So can we. It isn't easy. It is, in fact, very difficult. But there isn't a more glorious life in this earthly pilgrimage, and God tells us to "*... be strong and very courageous...*" (Joshua 1:7).

---

1 Sir Walter Scott, *Waverley* (Digireads.com Publishing, 2020), 5.

SECTION I:
BORN FOR A PURPOSE

chapter one

BEING JOSHUA

This book is about "being" Joshua. Who was this man? What was he? How did he become Joshua, Son of Nun, Moses's assistant, Moses's commander, Moses's successor? What happened? What did he do? What did God do?

We can start before Joshua's beginning. We often think our life as a believer began when we trusted Christ. There is a truth there. At that point, a new life was born in us and began to grow. Like the life of God in a man's soul, in Christ we became *"a new creation"* (1 Cor 5:17). That is without doubt a new beginning. However, God was working throughout our lives to bring us to the place of conversion. He was preparing us throughout life for His service.

Also, and less understood, God planned His purposes for us in eternity. Even before conception, God saw us and reasoned a purpose for us. He decided who we would be and included us in His great plan of salvation. Although we had freedom and choices to make in the process, we couldn't thwart the divine plan. Similarly, God's main purpose for Joshua was to lead Israel into the Promised Land. God fulfilled His plan. Joshua and Israel got there, and Israel is still there.

So, a fundamental attitude for believers is to acknowledge the fact that God has a purpose for them planned in eternity before our ancestors were born. You should know that God's plan has been working through generations, throughout your life, to bring you into the world in exactly the conditions God planned. It may seem that your life is unfolding in an apparently free way, but God will bring you to himself, and you will begin a journey with Him. He will unfold wonders for your life if you give your life wholly to Him. Everything that happens He can turn to good. If you follow Him, your life will be seen in eternity as a good life, filled with purpose to the glory of God. Your painful sorrows will be turned to joy, and your trials will be triumphs… in eternity.

Joshua's life has three big eras: slavery for forty years; the wilderness for forty years; then, the time of the Promised Land including warfare and statesman-like work, then a period of retirement. In total, thirty years in Canaan. He couldn't have had one without the others.

While this book will mostly keep to the topic, there also will be some worthwhile 'wanderings.' You will be encouraged to ask, "How does being me resemble being Joshua?" You will be encouraged to realize that you are brothers. You may also be terrified by the thought!

chapter two

BEING BORN

Joshua was born into Egyptian slavery around 1,500 BC… into the oppression that existed for four hundred years before him. The word "slave" is an insufficient description of a man made in the image of God. Yet slavery was the reality of his world from day one. Now, there's a start to life!

An ancient practice, slavery appears to have had a revival in the western world. This revival is a demon that we haven't been able to cast out. At times, it appears to be no more than a historical talking point. But even the best of civilizations have been unable to completely cast it out. Frequently, as in our day, it returns with "… *seven other spirits more wicked than himself…*" (Matt. 12:45). Despite this, most people talking about slavery today have never actually experienced it. For Joshua, it was his daily life. He was born a slave.

Little Joshua wasn't just a bunch of cells that came about by accident. He wasn't haphazard. Joshua's birth was an exciting, joyful hope!

Joshua's birth was also the result of divine deliberation, a plan with a divine purpose. He was conceived in the womb but created by the creator. "*So God created man in His own image; in the image of God He created him; male and female He created them*" (Genesis 1: 27). They were created for a purpose! Every life has a purpose. This understanding is the start of viewing life correctly: see yourself as a child of God, made in His image, born for a divine purpose. Humble or great? You have a say. Eternity will tell.

chapter three
BEING AWARE

This belief system wasn't the result of medical ignorance or superstition, as though conception overawed them. There was no need to manufacture some magical source for the miracle of a child. Neither men nor medical knowledge were as primitive as modern medicine would have us believe. People had an entirely sufficient understanding of natural events. While modern medicine can sometimes make birth safer, it has conspired to make a mother's womb the most dangerous place in the universe! Their judgement will be swift.

Adam and Eve delivered Cain and Abel on their own. Joseph and Mary delivered Christ into the world without assistance! They knew what was happening. They also knew it was unquestionably a miracle! Instead of overwhelming them into superstition, it served to confirm the wholesome and rational belief they had in God. A human being is an impressive, divine design. Tiny Joshua was designed and made in the image of God. A slave with no life of his own, certainly not what many might define as "a life." The circumstances justifying abortion are often luxurious when compared to slavery. In this, we declare ourselves to know nothing.

From the beginning of time, people have been born into poverty. Many beautiful, healthy babies have been born in the slums of Mumbai, the corruption of Cambodia, and under the scourge of Nazism. From the communist regimes of Russia and China throughout the 20th century, to the Western world with drugs and sex trafficking ... the list is endless. Slavery comes in many guises. Yet, even, and perhaps especially in these environments, parents stand in contradistinction to us today... they rejoiced and sang because, at the birth of a child, they were given hope. The Western world undoubtedly represents the greatest society that ever lived. Yet, we are afraid to bring a child into this world! We have so much to unlearn. We have embraced so many lies. But take courage… God has His Joshua's in preparation, in and out of the womb. You, dear reader, can be one of them.

chapter four

BEING GIVEN HOPE

This society of slaves rejoiced with uncontrollable mirth at Joshua's birth. As people have done in every society, good or bad, even before a child's birth parents embraced a compulsive optimism. From conception, they hoped that Joshua might be the one to deliver them. These Israelite slaves realized that, despite the circumstances, this 'newborn' could take them to glorious freedom, into the land God promised to Abraham. *Hope itself confers purpose, it reasons investment.* Joshua would see the fulfillment because, through him, God would deliver them into the Promised Land.

Very quickly, let me encourage and challenge you in this. *God's servants must deliver people into His promised land.* Have you ever led a soul to Christ? Are you ambitious to be something in the church of Jesus Christ? Make it your heart's desire to lead a sinner to Jesus soon! The church is full of believers who have never brought anybody to faith. They think they will fulfill the great commission by sending other people to "make disciples!"

Every newborn is a potential rejection of the parents' pain, a denial of the permanence of their 'slavery.' From the moment of Joshua's conception, his parents' view of their nation's four hundred years of slavery could be seen in a different light. Every child must be seen as having the potential to change everything for the better!

We can easily imagine Joshua's first cry as a war cry. It lasted his entire life. His life was a blessing to his nation and to the future of the world, a timeless example of how one child with God can be the solution to that which troubles us.

SECTION II:
EARLY LIFE AND LEARNING

chapter 5

BEING SOMETHING WHEN YOU ARE NOTHING

Joshua took his first gasp of God's free air and tasted freedom. His tiny wee voice cried out a defiant rejection of slavery. He refused attempts to be silent or still, he kicked and punched with his incoherent limbs until his hunger was satisfied. He struggled constantly until he became strong. He developed and grew, defied despair, and became a man much earlier in life than modern men do (still playing games in their thirties!). He learned to stand tall, even in slavish poverty.

How are you doing in your circumstances? Joshua was a man long before he became an adult. By the Exodus, he had grown in the knowledge of God's ways. Before the Exodus, he had also become a man of God.

The best people are the best in the worst circumstances! They are great long before they become anything. In the worst of circumstances, God's men choose to rise above everything by faith in Him. That's Joshua. Brother, sister, in your circumstances will you be a Joshua now? Right where you are is where you start to be a man of God.

Please note, it was in the providence of God that Joshua was born as a slave. Yet God embraced Joshua. That should encourage anyone with damaged self-esteem. God made Joshua the opposite of what men expected him to be. So many predictions made by men in the Bible regarding other men are wrong—Moses, David, and Christ Himself.

Evil, for Joshua, wasn't the whip master. Evil was seeing himself as the Egyptians saw him, as less than human. More to the point, evil for Joshua was seeing himself as less than a child of God. Joshua saw himself thus, despite his slavery. His whole being was an energetic, faith-filled rejection of the reality that was his life. Be like him!

God developed him and made him, first, a godly man. Then followed a whole list of achievements and accomplishments. All were built on the foundation of God in Joshua's life: a military commander of note, a nation builder, a spiritual leader, and a lovable character.

God's plan for your life might be a gloriously ordinary one, but it may equally be a gloriously awesome one. Some of that will be up to you. But not without divine help. If you will but walk with God, you will be something of note in eternity, maybe even in time. Be a man or a woman of God. Be a Joshua.

chapter six

BEING AWARE OF GOD

How did Joshua achieve this ability to see God in everything? How can we achieve this? One source is reading the Old Testament stories. Did you expect a more difficult challenge? Reading the Bible is a spiritual discipline. It isn't just reading a book. When the believer forgets to read with faith, they often turn to current literature, or they might return to the higher quality of past writers, but these won't profit them. The word of God, read with faithful anticipation and listening for the Holy Spirit, is food that Joshua benefitted from. If your Bible reading is mechanical, your life won't be inspired. Joshua was taught the Old Testament by parents whose faith aided Joshua's spiritual digestion. Joshua was fed on the Old Testament writings of his spiritual forefathers.

The more you understand the Bible, the more beneficial Bible college education will be if you desire to go there. Most believers never go to a Bible college. It is often simply a way to get certification of a certain level of Bible knowledge and associated subjects. It isn't designed to make you a man of God. I believe God wants His servants to be as educated as they can be, and the full range of studies available in the West are valuable. Although, as I write, many are seriously doubting the benefit of a liberal arts degree. However, becoming a man of God doesn't happen in a college. It happens in a normal life, with your head and heart engaged in a walk with God and your interest focussed inside the Bible.

For Joshua, this awareness of God in everything was present in the normal events of life: by the fireside, at the dinner table, and at times and seasons of the year. Joshua learned in a home environment, under an authority that was respected. Teaching was lived out in the real world.

At times, freedom must have seemed like a fairy tale… a promised land, a great nation… what was that to young Joshua the slave? It was about believing faith! Plus, Joshua had the convincing example of family and friends. Have you ever felt that the Bible might not resonate with your teenagers in this fascinating world? How do you think Joshua's parents had the confidence to impress Joshua with the hope of a "promised land?" Their strength came from their active faith in God. Without evidence of faith, no teenager will be moved. Do you have it? Do you nurture it by Bible reading and prayer? Do you introduce your children to other believing families? Do they hear you praying, see you worshipping, observe your faith under the whiplash of life?

The influence of Joshua's parents, and the whole society of slaves, was such that the patriarchs were the heroes of Joshua's young life. Joshua wanted to be like them. Do you?

What a successful generation! Joshua understood that God wanted to have fellowship with His children. He loved them. Joshua realized that God didn't see him as men did, a slave. God saw Joshua as the man who would assist Moses in the desert wanderings. Who do you want to be like? The great Old Testament figures are there to draw us after the Lord. They are waiting in the pages of the Bible to teach us. Are you listening to them? Joshua was.

Like the patriarchs, Joshua learned to see God in everything. This isn't just a superficial mind game—it results in a real change of worldview. He believed in God. Everyone who believes in God has a sense of destiny. Every man, woman or child, born-again by God's Holy Spirit, should sense a godly purpose to some extent.

chapter seven

FAITH + PAIN = PREPARATION

Joshua was familiar with the patriarchs, so he must have understood that suffering was intrinsic with preparation for God's service. Abraham left his home and went to a land he didn't know, leaving the familiar aspects of life behind. What loneliness! And what are we to make of this: "*... he went out, not knowing where he was going...*" (Heb. 11:8). What faith! Abraham was called to sacrifice his only son, believing that God could raise him up again. What sacrifice! God stopped Abraham, "*And He said, 'Do not lay your hand on the lad, or do anything to him; for now I know that you fear God, since you have not withheld your son, your only son, from Me'*" (Genesis 22:12).

Later, we discover Jacob, who, at the depth of despair, held on to the angel all night and received the blessing:

> *But he said, "I will not let You go unless You bless me!" So, He said to him, "What is your name?" He said, "Jacob." And He said, "Your name shall no longer be called Jacob, but Israel; for you have struggled with God and with men, and have prevailed."*
>
> —Gen 32:26–28

Yes, what a struggle Jacob had his whole life!

Joshua understood the principle that pain has a purpose. Difficulties are designed to teach us about ourselves and the Lord. When in trouble, turn to Him, not just for help but for grace to submit and learn.

When they beat Joshua, he received the lashes as having a purpose from an all-powerful, all-good God. He accepted his state as temporary—believing God could and would deliver him in His time. None of us naturally accept trouble from the hand of God. We find other sources to blame including ourselves. The believer is less interested in blame, more interested in purpose. The believer asks questions like *what is the Lord teaching me?* What can I learn here? How can I respond in a way that glorifies God? Joshua learned these principles in the furnace of life. Are you willing to learn like this? Do you want to be like Joshua? Or Jesus? Then take a different view of suffering.

Was this attitude unrealistic? Dear reader, 'faith' by its very nature appears unrealistic, especially if you take God out of the mix. However, Joshua believed that God reigned in the affairs of men. "*… that the living may know that the Most High rules in the kingdom of men…*" (Daniel 4:17). There is no other way to view trouble. Every generation must learn this.

Joshua's name meant "salvation," and he believed God would save. The nation of Israel as slaves held on to their faith—truth is… it was God who held on to them! They are still with us today. We can learn from them in the scriptures.

Imagine telling your difficulty to Joshua, in his role as a slave. Tell me, would he sympathize with you? He certainly would. But then he might also rebuke you and shake you…

God made His people to be survivors, like Joshua, like the heroes in Hebrews 11, people who rejected failure, misery, and defeat. We, the people of God, are His delight, and we survive as Joshua did. God's name is still revered and declared over our newborn—'God Saves'—that's what Joshua means. This was spoken over Joshua the slave… Joshua the spy… and Joshua the man of God before Jericho—the man of God throughout life and even on his deathbed. Listen to his life. Let it speak to you as you read. Whoever you are, God can make you a Joshua. You will keep your name. You will be yourself, not acting, not a clone. God wants you as you are. But He will change you.

chapter eight

BEING A FUNCTIONING SOCIETY OF SLAVES

Born Yeshua the Son of Nun, Moses renamed him Joshua. He had never known freedom. It is fair to suggest that he saw friends and relatives die in abject misery. What age was he when he felt the whip for the first time? What age was he when he chose to live and not give up? When he decided to give himself to the Lord seriously? You don't have to be old to do that. You can be serious about God all your life. Those who are most successful at godliness, don't get caught up in themselves. They are caught up with Jesus.

His parents were probably strong in their faith. The teaching of the home can only be fairly assessed in eternity. Many parents' good teaching is only seen in grandchildren. Joshua seems to have listened because at around forty he became Moses's assistant.

A strange thing, is it not, that we aren't given intricate details of Israel's life in Egypt. There aren't graphic depictions of cruelty. The 20th-century Holocaust was six long years, and there are countless stories of heroics, bravery, and suffering. But for four hundred years in Egypt there is no record of exploits or of great heroes. The four hundred years has only one message: they were slaves.

The introductory line is that after the death of Joseph, "…there arose a new king over Egypt, who did not know Joseph" (Exodus 1:8). Into this vacuum came centuries of slavery. Joshua quickly experienced the loss of any comforts. Men negatively identifying other men is an ancient art. In the case of the new Egyptian king with Israel, it was done through fear. The motives behind disliking another person have been given many names, but it requires no rationale. It is a potent declaration of the sinful nature. Pastor beware!

That's all it takes—one individual in a large church can make your life miserable—unless you remember that God is in control. Beware of this fact.

Change can never be ruled out, and change can be unpredictable. A new 'king' might be a new partner, a new job, a new political leader, or a new pastor. Indeed, a new season in life might usher in a hurricane of good or bad. Keep your trust and hope in God. The psalmist teaches us how to talk to ourselves in such moments, *"Why are you cast down, O my soul? And why are you disquieted within me? Hope in God…"* (Psalm 42:5).

And yet in all these circumstances, life must go on, and for Joshua it did. Young Joshua had to determine who he was for himself. He had choices. He could have merged into nothingness; he could have thoughtlessly hoped of the best. Some would have desperately tried to hide or scrabble a living like a dog. Many would have become bland, or bitter, or become an atheist and blame God—atheism can be bitterness expressed as unbelief. Men sometimes choose atheism when they most need God. The backslider is a prime example.

Joshua may have had such moments of reflection although they aren't mentioned. Joshua is presented as a man of constant, dependable faith in God. As we read, we recognize his devotion from his youth. That upbringing, the family one-on-one teaching through the years, worked! It bore fruit for a lifetime. If you are a home-schooler, be encouraged.

Israel functioned as slaves within an oppressive heathen nation. Their only certainty was that God had chosen them.

> *For you are a holy people to the Lord your God; the Lord your God has chosen you to be a people for Himself, a special treasure above all the peoples on the face of the earth. The Lord did not set His love on you nor choose you because you were more in number than any other people, for you were the least of all peoples; but because the Lord loves you…*
>
> —Deut. 7:6,7

Election doesn't make us proud. It is a humbling teaching. It reminds us that we were nothing at all... Yet the Lord chose to set His love upon us. What an amazing thing! Remember this truth when the devil says you aren't good enough... tell him you know that better than he does, and so does God... but He still chose you.

SECTION III:
MOSES AND THE EXODUS

chapter nine

DESERTS BEING SPRINGBOARDS

Moses fled to the desert and stayed there for forty years. God's deliverer, Moses, was hiding in the desert! However, God was working in Moses's heart in the silent sand dunes of the desert. It was in this time that Joshua was born into slavery. Young Joshua and Moses were brought close to the Lord during this time. Moses was restored in the heat of the desert. Joshua was matured in the heat of slavery. Can you believe that your present circumstances are exactly what you need to become what God wants you to be? They are—grasp them. Get in harmony with what God is doing in your life.

God's timing is perfect, but we often fail to synchronize with Him! These long years worked many things into both Moses and Joshua. When Moses returns, in God's perfect timing, Joshua is a man. After they escape Egypt, but before they are attacked by Amalek, Joshua became Moses's assistant. Joshua presumably came to Moses's attention during the time in the desert. For some time, Joshua had a quiet reputation. He probably was unaware of it himself, but it reached Moses.

Their two lives demonstrate a perfect preparedness for that which God purposed, the Exodus! Could God have been preparing you for just such a time as this? A time that you don't even see coming or imagine? But you may be praying for it to happen.

Many of God's dear children have been in 'deserts' for decades. Many churches likewise have become dry ghettos where believers have carved out a lifestyle they think is close to heaven. But it's not, they should be on a war footing. Many sermons have been preached trying to awaken believers, often by a visiting preacher when the pastor had given in to discouragement. Books have been written to try to make us think harder, to see ourselves in a better light than mere 'world watchers' who do nothing but talk. Books written on revival have been a powerful influence for individuals and churches, often presenting God's people as the "dry bones" in Ezekiel's valley.

A few revivals of great significance have happened in modern times. In 1906, in Los Angeles under the ministry of Rev. J. Seymour, the Azusa Street revival gave birth to the movement called Pentecostalism. Around the same time, 1904–1905, the Welsh revival awakened the church under Owen Roberts in the United Kingdom. Later, the Hebridean Revival occurred on the islands off the west coast of Scotland mid-20th century. These revivals had a tremendous influence on the church of their day, which was arguably backslidden and offering no gospel to the world. It isn't possible to read these accounts and remain satisfied with your present state before God. It's impossible to deny the need that exists today. Revival doesn't make anybody rich or famous! Revival makes men repent. Revival begins by making God's people weep before they sing!

In this time as you read, perhaps you have given up? Have you fallen into a purposeless desert? Perhaps you know this to be true but don't know what to do. Stand up, grasp your situation by faith, and *"...forgetting those things which are behind and reaching forward to those things which are ahead..."* (Philippians 3:13). Believe God is in control and has a divine purpose. Then, get right with God and get back into a Bible believing church, begin again to pray and to feed on God's Word and fellowship with the Lord's people. Then be amazed as God turns your pain into purpose, your failures into lessons learned.

> *Serve the Lord with gladness; Come before His presence with singing. Know that the Lord, He is God; It is He who has made us, and not we ourselves; We are His people and the sheep of His pasture Enter into His gates with*

thanksgiving, And into His courts with praise. Be thankful to Him, and bless His name.

—Psalm 100:2–4

God prepared Moses for his calling in a desert to lead His people through a desert. He brought Joshua into slavery to instill such a passion for freedom that he took God's people from that desert right into Canaan, the Promised Land! He can use you, too.

chapter ten

THE GOSPEL IN EXODUS

Joshua saw Moses burst onto the royal scene in Egypt. Suddenly there were plagues. He saw the River Nile turn blood red, saw his father slay the best lamb and apply its blood to the doorposts of their humble abode. Joshua partook of the very first Passover. He sat silently as the Angel of Death passed over his home. No doubt he remembered that moment—the sigh of peace in the land of Goshen, uncomfortably contrasted by the harrowing lament of the Egyptians. The Bible allows for rejoicing in our victories and delighting at God's deliverance. Yet it doesn't allow us to gloat over human suffering. Rejoicing in divine judgements carries a legitimate caution because of our human kinship.

Surely Joshua sensed an uncomfortable relief as the angel of death passed on, and he and his family remained unharmed, protected by the blood of the lamb. Did he wonder why he was spared? Did he understand later, in some hazy way, that the blood of the sacrificial lamb foreshadowed another sacrifice that would be the cost of his eternal salvation? Like Adam and Eve before him, as God made them coats of skins to cover their nakedness and shame? Did they too wonder what this meant? We know that both instances are prophetic symbols, as John the Baptist cried out: "*...Behold the Lamb of God which taketh away the sin of the world*" (John 1:29). Joshua experienced God's judgement passing over his head. Having suffered under oppression, he knew that God's judgements were justified and righteous.

Here, in Joshua's youth, we have God setting fundamental gospel truths: sin produces death. The life of the flesh is in the blood.

The extent to which they understood this is unknown. It's as though they were seeing through a veil. Sufficient to say, the Old Testament saints understood essential things about God and essential things about man. They realized that men couldn't be saved merely by the blood of animals, but they knew it was a picture of their real salvation still to come. In the book of Hebrews, the writer says, *"For it is not possible that the blood of bulls and goats could take away sins"* (Heb 10:4). This is a fundamental statement of truth. The Old Testament pictures were, and still are, suggestive of the shedding of the blood of Christ. Their sins, like ours, were cleansed by Christ's blood.

The Old Testament saints couldn't see Calvary approaching 1,500 years after Joshua. We are two thousand years after Calvary. We have it all written down for us to read freely. Did you know that your salvation was purchased by the blood of Christ? Do you understand that because Jesus suffered in your place salvation is a gift from God, to be accepted by faith? Salvation couldn't be purchased any other way. Our good deeds, our religious attendance, church membership, status in society or church… are like filthy rags in His sight. *"But we are all like an unclean thing, and all our righteousnesses are like filthy rags; we all fade as a leaf; and our iniquities, like the wind, have taken us away."* (Isaiah 64:6).

Joshua would never forget that night in Egypt. We must never forget the blood of Christ. We dare not wander from it, or we lose our essential identity as the people of God. All revivals are a return to Jesus as the centre, the core, the essence, of our identity as believers. Those who wish to serve God must be captured by Jesus and held by His love. They must never let the experience fade.

This is fundamental to Christian leadership. We need to understand how His suffering is laid out in the Old Testament, and how the New Testament interprets the Old in this respect. We must be convinced that this is God's revelation of salvation in the Old Testament. The New Testament holds Old and New Testament saints together as one. By the word "saint," we understand, "ordinary believer."

The pastor can see himself like Joshua and Moses. Understand that by the preaching of the Word he will see God redeem people from slavery to sin, taking them into a land filled with milk and honey. All the things experienced by God's leaders in the past are potentially ours in kind. What a privilege to have a Bible!

chapter eleven
BEING RE-DEFINED

Four hundred years in Egypt defined the nation of Israel. It was a simple one-word definition: *slaves*. That definition was obliterated by the Exodus. They never forgot this, and to this day their remembrance of it is celebrated. The experience of coming to Christ should have similar results for us. Being reconciled to God should be our defining moment—renewed and refreshed weekly, "often", by the Lord's table. And it should relegate our past into a silent mist. God can remove our past altogether.

All the dealings between God and His people are defining moments. Though some experiences may be more profound than others, all the acts of God work to fix our faith upon Him and bring us closer to Him. They also lift us out from under the sins of others, at least in a spiritual sense. Oppressive circumstances may persist, but we are set free from bondage internally. Joshua was lifted out of slavery in a short, but life-changing, series of events summed up in one word: 'Exodus!' Come to Jesus today and experience your own exodus, your own deliverance from whatever the problem is keeping you from walking with Jesus Christ.

Many believers allow themselves to remain in their 'Egypt,' their 'slavery.' This might be a birthplace, poverty, ignorance, or it could be a broken home, or a broken relationship. A hurt in a church? There isn't a hint that four hundred years of slavery left any negative influence on the life of Joshua. He left slavery. It gave him nothing good to remember, so he forgot it. But this amazing thing, being able to forget, was apparently easy for Joshua because a greater thing happened. The Exodus was a more powerful defining moment—it brought Joshua and the nation of Israel into *"...the glorious liberty of the children of God"* (Romans 8:21)! Seek it, find Him today!

Every leader must recognize and remember these moments in their lives and the lives of others. Visit them when you need encouragement. You won't be so reliant on pastors' conferences if you have regular dealings with God. There's no substitute for a sound gospel. It produces sound converts; they have been re-defined, recreated in the image of Christ.

The Exodus established Joshua's sense of worth. It didn't make him proud. Joshua realized that God chose both Israel and him. The same applies to every believer. Our sense of worth doesn't come from anything good in us. Only God's free, undeserving grace defines us, and it lifts us to heaven. This gift through Christ is what makes us fit for fellowship with God.

This series of books is about being believers. *Being Joseph...* and *Being Ruth...* as believers. *Being Joshua*, is also about Joshua being a believer. Our entire being, who we are, as 'believers,' is based upon the fact that God so loved us that He gave His only Son for us.

Joshua understood the sacrificial nature of God's plan of salvation. He understood it enough to recognize that he and his nation were special to God. They didn't understand it fully, yet they walked by faith. We too must believe that: *"For God so loved the world that He gave His only begotten Son, that whoever believes in Him should not perish but have everlasting life"* (John 3:16).

The Old Testament saints were saved the same way as New Testament saints—by believing faith. This was Joshua's family background, his childhood and youth leading to adulthood. It's quite an awesome experience, in the old-fashioned sense of being filled with awe. Wouldn't you agree?

chapter twelve
PROBLEMS BEING PROPELLANTS

So then, quite early in the life of Joshua, while not mentioned in the narrative, we find him at the Red Sea watching Moses, *"...the Man of God"* (Deut. 33:1). The Red Sea was before them, the Egyptian army in full pursuit behind them. Geographically, there was no escape route. What would you have done? They panicked. They began accusing Moses and by implication, God Himself! They cried out, *"... it would have been better for us to serve the Egyptians than that we should die in the wilderness"* (Exodus 14:12). This accusation is the logic of unbelief! It has no God in its thinking. Israel couldn't see a way out, so they concluded that there was no way out. How like them we are! Joshua was there. He perhaps learned that when men are in trouble, they blame their leaders. Many pastors have had to "move on" because it was decided that their departure would solve a problem. Sometimes the people may have been right. Many more times they have been wrong.

Difficulty comes, and we search for a way to circumvent it. In the story of the Red Sea, God sent the problem in the first place and intended the problem to be the way of deliverance. Like a gas propellant carries the cleaner to the mechanism, so problems can carry us to where God wants us to be. God sends problems to bring us to Himself as a matter of principle. The Sea was the problem. The sea was also the means of deliverance. The Sea was also the means of judgement on their enemies. Moses addressed the problem and the complaint—and Joshua was listening.

Moses said, *"Do not be afraid, Stand Still and see the salvation of the Lord... the Lord will fight for you, and you shall hold your peace"* (Exodus 14: 13,14). And we know the rest, how God opened the Red Sea and delivered His people without them doing anything other than to have a fascinating walk through the sea on dry land! When God ends your slavery, it is done, finished. There is no lingering Egyptian problem. It's dead. However, note that every major deliverance is challenged soon after it is accomplished. Joshua was taking it all in.

There are many ways to listen. We can hear but not 'listen,' refusing to accept what is said. We can ignore something before hearing the whole story. For the believer, listening is essentially an act of faith. Joshua engaged God by listening with faith. He heard Moses speak but he also heard another voice—the voice of God spoke in Joshua's heart affirming what Moses said. Joshua personalized and sanctified the moment. When Moses spoke at the Red Sea, Joshua recognized a moment to be obeyed, remembered, and hallowed. Joshua actually walked through the Red Sea on dry ground!

chapter thirteen
LISTENING WITH FAITH

Your pastor is communicating in the same 'character' as Moses. Every ministry session and worship gathering is intended for us to hear God's message and soak its principles into our souls by actively listening, engaging in faith.

We must learn to grasp God's Word by faith. The aim isn't to *learn* as much as to *realize* His truth in our hearts. Each sermon is a moment to be grasped and not missed. Sermons aren't classroom teaching sessions. The purpose is to engage the believer with God, right there and then by faith, in the same way Moses instructed Israel, there and then, to stand still at the Red Sea. Imagine what would have been missed if you postponed the realization?! Just a few hours later, the Red Sea returned to its appointed place and death was all it offered. Grasp the moment!

Joshua is taught by Moses how the believer should respond to the impossible. Especially where God's honour is at stake. Especially when the problem is a direct consequence of obedience. Obedience often produces its own unique problems! Joshua learned not to let fear father unbelief.

When Moses said, "Stand still," he intended a calming disposition, a moment of suspension. A silencing of the noise that fills our head when we are afraid. A moment conveyed in these words of the psalmist, *"Be still and know that I am God"* (Psalm 46:10). I wonder if Joshua exercised such faith and brought all the turmoil inside him under the control of his conviction that Jehovah is God! Thereby, settling in under the wings of the Almighty and soaking up the experience. Or maybe he had already learned this skill at the Passover.

He might have already been fully comfortable having exercised faith every time an Egyptian master approached him in Egypt. God gives us experiences to prepare us for the 'real' thing when it comes. His aim is to "prove us," not to fail us.

When you don't know what to do, "... *hold your peace*" (Exodus 14:14). Peace in times like these is likely to fly away. Rest in the Lord until God brings the deliverance.

Sometimes God's peace comes to control us. More often we must control our peace by faith.

Faith silences all the protestations of fear. Faith that actively holds on to God can extend a silent calm. When Israel is told to hold their peace, we must understand it meant more than a mere refusal to scream!

Joshua listened, saw these principles in action, and embraced them. When the present-day reader reads the Old Testament stories, he or she, young or old, should also grasp them as Joshua did, and let God sink them into their very being. When we read and learn this attitude of faith, we become men and women of God, like Joshua was by the time this matter came to be.

Many sit under the sound of God's Word every week, yet are never changed. What they expect from a morning service is out of balance. They expect to enjoy worship. They expect to be educated. They expect to feel something. Sadly, some expect nothing at all! They have never asked "By what mechanism does preaching change us?" There is only one mechanism that can take truth and actuate it in the heart. That mechanism is believing faith practiced by the hearer!

Listen then with faith to the writer to the Hebrews: "*For indeed the gospel was preached to us as well as to them; but the word which they heard did not profit them, not being mixed with faith in those who heard it*" (Hebrews 4:2). The enemy of our souls isn't concerned about us understanding truth or even about our interest level. He knows that neither interest nor understanding makes truth work in the believer. *Only*... believing, appropriating faith, produces the end intended by God, a life fashioned into the image of Christ. Anything that might detract from such engagement is to be avoided.

However, this faith and listening isn't fragile. It is robust, focussed and intentional. It is a faith that works. This kind of faith produces visible results that have life and vigour. Such faith sustains the believer. It enabled Joshua to walk right through the Red Sea on dry land!

A key verse in the Red-Sea crossing is the verse which says, "*...so the people feared the Lord...*" (Exod. 14:31). Surely fear was a normal response to what just happened. Joshua was there, looking, involved, and he too learned again the fear of the Lord, the beginning of wisdom. This wisdom, this fear, is essential for the pastor or church leader. Best to have developed it before we are in the pulpit or an elders' meeting. Every time we exercise faith and see God's answer, we learn the fear of the Lord and become wiser.

There is no prior wisdom! It is the absolute beginning of godly wisdom. It occurs before we come to a conscious faith in Christ. It causes the sinner to run to Jesus, for safety, and for salvation: a healthy fear resulting in wise action.

SECTION IV:
BEING A WANDERER

chapter fourteen

BEING IN THE DESERT

To further grasp Joshua, we must find him in the wilderness. We will look at Joshua where he appears, or is implicated, in the wilderness years.

If you know someone in their 'wilderness' experience, you know them in depth, more than a mere coffee and chat. If you saw them under pressure or pain, you would have seen them in a deeper state than everyday life. Abnormal, or extreme life experiences produce different responses, a deeper outlook to events. This is true in both natural and spiritual life.

Men who came through the Second World War were affected for the rest of their lives. Men who came through the Lewis revival were changed for the rest of their lives. The best evidence for my case, of course, is the disciples. Once a man walks with Jesus, he is never the same again.

We want to see Joshua in his "wilderness." We are told little about him as a slave. In the wilderness accounts, we see more of him. At this point in the narrative, Joshua's life has been filled with God's miraculous interventions, but God isn't merely interested in big interventions.

Before Amalek, Israel saw water flow from a rock and manna drop from heaven on the ground for them to eat. Note that when Jesus gives his disciples a pattern for praying, He tells them to pray *"Give us this day our daily bread..."* (Matt. 6:11). In the wilderness, God demonstrated His ability to do just that! Israel was fed every morning in the desert for forty years. Joshua tasted this miracle every day. The man of God must eat heavenly food every day. Joshua also learned how to discern where complaints were to be directed.

Many church leaders try to deal with everything to make themselves look efficient or wage-worthy. They try to solve all the problems. However, God likes to be involved in His church too! Joshua learned how to do this here. He learned to leave the Lord some room in the life of the people, to intervene and show His love and power on their behalf. Remember that you are on dangerous ground if you consider that you are the redeemer of God's church in any sense at all. In life's deserts, learn that you are limited, God is not.

chapter fifteen
AMALEK REPULSED

And so, Israel leaves Egypt, walking out towards the Red Sea. They didn't have to swim or build boats or defend their position. The Red Sea just opened like a dream, allowing Israel to cross into freedom. Joshua was free. Soon they were travelling through the desert learning God's ways as they journeyed. But freedom brought its own problems! Exodus 17:8 tells us that Amalek came and fought with Israel at Rephidim.

Moses appointed Joshua to lead Israel against Amalek. We can fairly assume that Moses had been observing Joshua and seen his character and ability. Above all, Moses must have seen Joshua's faith and trust in God. Moses knew Joshua could lead the army to victory, but we aren't told how Joshua felt. It didn't really matter. It only mattered that he obeyed.

Amalek was coming, armed and angry. Joshua had to step up and fight! Joshua shows us how God makes men out of boys! God also, as an aside, turns quiet girls into women of God. This isn't a fashion or a rebellion. God doesn't turn women into the image of grubby men! It's a conversion to Jesus Christ. He made them strong to stand before an angry world while still being who they were, wives, mothers, daughters, and grandmothers, remaining thoroughly the gentler sex. Yet women of God fought evil and won souls for Christ all over the world. Their exploits are written in the history of the church since early times for all to read. But while women are called to walk with God, men are also called to lead by faith and example. Are you one of those men? Joshua was, and in this story, we have his first military battle.

Men had been fighting battles for centuries. They had it down to a fine art. Everybody on the battlefield was familiar with the weapons of war. Let's look at the state of Israel before this battle. They were in a time of inner conflict, a time of division. They desperately needed to be united. What should happen in this situation? Time out? There was no 'time' to take out.

Exodus 17:7 tells us that the place where Israel had come to was called Massah and Meribah because of *"contention"* within Israel. In the distracted confusion, Amalek came to fight against Israel. Whenever the Lord's people are in contention with Him or one another, the devil sees an opportunity. Pastors are often embroiled in such situations. But we must learn to remain spiritually alert because a bigger problem might come, as Amalek came against Israel.

Now, an external threat is often a good incentive to fix internal problems. Many a king or a politician started a foreign war to distract from domestic failure. In this story, we are told that Israel had no time to fix this division. Joshua told Israel to choose men to fight—tomorrow! They did, and they won because God fought for them. Many would have doubted Moses's wisdom in sending Joshua to battle with a divided army. Many church leaders would see the need for divisions to be healed before the summer outreach or the annual mission trip. The disunity didn't hinder Joshua. He created an army and was ready to fight within twenty-four hours.

chapter sixteen

BEING IN PRAYER

The fight seems to have dissipated the division. We hear no more about it—because of the victory won. Note how the victory was accomplished. Joshua led the army. But Moses, Aaron, and Hur went up to the top of the hill where they could see the battle. There Moses held up his hands and Israel prevailed. When Moses's arms became tired, Aaron and Hur sat him on a rock, and they raised Moses's hands. Again, Israel prevailed. Joshua won the battle but not without the action of these three accomplices.

A.W. Pink in his book *Gleanings in Exodus*, points out that this is best seen as a picture of believing prayer among God's people. Moses is helped by Aaron and Hur. He quotes 1 Timothy 2:8 that men ought to "*... pray everywhere, lifting up holy hands, without wrath and doubting.*" Pink says Aaron, being the head of the priestly class, represents Christ, our high priest, indicating the help we will receive as He intercedes for us in heaven when our praying hands begin to falter. He goes on to suggest that Hur, whose name means "light," represents the divine Holy Spirit in His help for us here in this life on earth. Pink quotes Romans 8:26 "*Likewise the Spirit also helps in our weaknesses... The Spirit Himself makes intercession for us with groanings which cannot be uttered.*" Pink elaborates widely on this idea quoting many texts and making many connections.[2]

What he says is a wonderful exposition of the scriptures. He says much more than I have quoted on this event. For this book, we would benefit simply from the recognition that: "*Two are better*

---

2   Arthur W. Pink, *Gleaning in Exodus* (Chicago: Moody Press, 1974).

than one, Because they have a good reward for their labor. For if they fall, one will lift up his companion. But woe to him who is alone when he falls, For he has no one to help him up... And a threefold cord is not quickly broken" (Eccles. 4:9,10,12). To move too quickly into typology takes us away from the scripture which is, after all, about four men. Three of whom can easily be seen praying while the fourth is seen as benefitting in his service for the Lord and His people. Joshua is our focus, though we see him closely working with Moses, Aaron, and Hur. Pink helpfully points out that prayer isn't just a human endeavour. God the Holy Spirit and God the Son are both intimately involved when we pray, and still involved, if differently, when we don't.

chapter seventeen
BEING WRITTEN DOWN

Finally, this part of the story. The Lord told Moses: "*Write this for a memorial in the book and recount it in the hearing of Joshua...*" (Exodus 17:14). We might wonder why? Records should be kept of God's victories over our enemies then and now. Moses recounted it to Joshua in order to have the record confirmed. Oral and written records went together on many occasions in the Bible, this being such a case. A church business meeting might be a more edifying place if we included a record of prayers asked and answered, with witnesses testifying to the veracity of the written report.

Their approach to recording was sophisticated. This is also seen in many other places in the Bible. They were careful to be accurate and give glory to God for His work. This should increase our confidence in the scriptures. Often it is criticized by those who don't understand the strictures associated with oral traditions, ancient and modern. Oral traditions still exist today. Here we have a brief insight into the care taken to record the works of God accurately, written down, read to an eyewitness, confirmed, and remembered. This record was preserved, and both written and oral recordings were passed down in families and national events through centuries with reverence and care. During this awesome process, lives were given to protect the story. Kings and caves were enlisted to aid the procession of God's Word through the centuries right to this day. The Bible has had enemies in every generation, yet God has preserved it, and it remains the bestselling book of all time... Have confidence in it. In my two pastorates I gave individuals the task of writing the church's history and producing a book. It was a great blessing in both cases. It used to be the normal practice in churches. They were a record of the works of God.

Now there is something else in this subject of passing down truth. The truth about our own dealings with God should also be part of our conversations in daily life. Men who have been dealt with by God have memories of these events. They don't go away. We should be telling our children and passing on this history in sermons and home visits, at hospital beds, and in the daily routines of life. Have you such tales? Anyone who sets out to serve God will acquire them as time goes on. The first such dealing is that the work of God the Holy Spirit brings us to Christ, having first brought us to repentance and faith. Receiving Jesus Christ is unforgettable! This one encounter with God is the foundation of all other encounters. It is first and foremost. Make sure you have met Him!

chapter eighteen
BEING READY TO FIGHT

Joshua was ready to fight. How might we assess if we are ready for a spiritual battle? Well surely our appetite for personal Bible reading, meditation, and study, would be a significant parameter? We teach our children verses like 2 Timothy 2:15: *"Study to shew yourself approved unto God, a workman that needeth not to be ashamed, rightly dividing the word of truth"* (KJV). This wasn't written for a child but for a young man called to be a pastor! So don't give up! Start reading daily. Read the Bible as though it was your "sword" and your life depended upon it.

Perhaps the saddest comment on the church, in terms of a measure of spirituality, is its corporate prayer life. Until the church reinstates prayer as one of its top priorities, we can't be taken seriously. We are unable to fight.

Prayer is the breath of the soul. No breath indicates no life. Singing, emotion, chatting, smiling, being nice, none of these indicate spiritual life. Prayer indicates spiritual life. A church culture that has minimal prayer is just a culture… Prayer is fundamental to who we are, to our very being. Let John Bunyan tell the hard truth. He said, "… You are not a praying man? You are not a Christian!"[3] Don't give up, start today and build on it daily until your whole being is wrapped up in prayer. My next book will be on "The Lord's Prayer." If you have an interest to serve God's people, you will have to have a 'prayer life'… better, would be to have a 'life of prayer.'

---

3 John Bunyan's *A Discourse Touching Prayer*, Accessed from: https://Biblesnet.com/John%20Bunyan%20A%20Discourse%20Touching%20Prayer.pdf

There is no substitute for prayer. Some, but not all, of the most theologically sound churches have the deadest prayer meetings. This has been an observation that has both troubled and puzzled me as a member of such otherwise wonderful churches. Prayer is a discipline. It is work. It is essential to spiritual life. If you want to be a leader in God's church, prayer must be your being. Prayer must be who you are!

Joshua's battle was only twenty-four hours away. Are you ready? Your next battle might be sooner. Joshua was ready to unite this divided people and take them to victory. Are you in a state of readiness to stand for the gospel, to lead a church? What are the Christian's battles? Is there such a thing as Christian warfare? Yes, there is. Do we have enemies? Yes, we do. Are our enemies flesh and blood? Generally, no—but yes, we have enemies. Well, Christian battles are spiritual battles. Spiritual warfare is a war against the soul of the believer. There may be a physical element to a spiritual battle. Christian warfare is nevertheless not about fists or guns. It is often about words, more often about deeds, and always about the Glory of God. We are God's ambassadors, His mouthpiece in a foreign state. The church has become dumb. There isn't a voice in the marketplace or in the corridors of power, no prophetic cry in the streets because there's no cry at the throne of God. There is no agony in the church today. Men slip into hell without a tear on the church's cheek. No prayer means hardened hearts. No prayer equals no breath, no voice, no life! If only we could grasp the truth, that a silent church has a terrifying and troubling effect! It isn't neutral.

We often keep silent to not upset people. The result is that humanity has lost its conscience! The world has become dark because the believer's lights have been hidden! (Matthew 5:15) This isn't what we had hoped for in 'holding our peace.' The world hears no restraining voice, no cautious warning call, and sadly no demand for repentance before God. They aren't aware of anybody who regards them as evil. They have no concept of evil. Their persistent, mind-numbing sinfulness is aided by the church's indulgent, numbing fear of man. When the church is silent, men's consciences are silent. They feel free to sin with impunity. And they do!

The church has ceased to be the conscience of the world. God's Ambassadors have become so unused to speaking out that when the odd one does, the voice is squeaky, and out of use. It does not convince, it is embarrassing, irrelevant. If in a fit of spiritual zeal, some young, strong voice is heard, the church itself goes into shock because it doesn't recognize the voice of its own ambassador. It simply marginalizes the voice for its own comfort. The church was first to use the weapon now described as 'cancel culture.' It does this in the name of 'peace,' which is often akin to death. One might sympathize if the New Testament's battles were physical like Joshua's. But they aren't physical. They are spiritual. We are without excuse! Amalek was Joshua's first military battle after the Exodus, and the Lord gave him victory.

SECTION V:
MOUNTAINS AND MEN

chapter nineteen
BEING ALONE

Exodus 24:13 tells us, "*So Moses arose with his assistant Joshua, and Moses went up to the mountain of God.*" It isn't clear how far Joshua went up the mountain, probably helping Moses with the climb. It is unlikely Joshua was at the top; he was likely partway up the mountain, and he waited there until Moses returned.

Joshua waited in silence somewhere between where God instructed Moses and where the people were about to worship a golden calf. Joshua wasn't in the presence of God with Moses, and not in the presence of the people. What went through Joshua's mind in that protracted silence? Surely this wasn't wasted time for Joshua. God often uses quiet moments to work in us. Waiting is a regular part of how God deals with us. We must learn to wait on Him. Solitude is used by God to speak comfort and strength.

His presence is always in perfect chronological harmony with His providence. God's presence is a timeless timepiece. Everything functions right in His presence.

Being on a mountain alone for a significant period can be helpful. Get out of the city as often as you can. Joshua appears to have been there for many days. I wonder if God brought him into this lonely place to work in his heart. There are many examples in the Bible of men brought to places just like Joshua. The experience of nature declaring the glory of God in 'surround sound' is a natural environment for us to meet with God.

This can be a monumental moment for the believer who is serious about God. The examples are prolific. From Moses in the desert to Joshua looking over Jericho; both Ruth and Naomi on the long, silent walk to back to Bethlehem; David on many occasions; Nehemiah on a late-night horseback ride through the desolate city; Job's entire existence for a prolonged period was abject isolation. Isaiah in the day that King Uzziah died. This pattern repeats throughout the Old Testament to the New, including Jesus being tempted in the desert, or in the garden, alone, praying.

Lonely moments are part of the lives of men dealing with God and God dealing with men, and even God dealing with God... in the garden of Gethsemane! Paul was forsaken by all but a few. Jonah, now there is an example to ponder! And what of the aged apostle John—in exile on Patmos hearing a voice behind him! These men would testify that their solitary moments became a meeting place with God. While pastors are generally fond of company, they must learn to love the solitary place, to search it out and make it their meeting place, like I am imagining Joshua on the mountain.

It was perfectly fitting for Joshua to wait there... to be alone with God. How can solitude ever be a problem to such a believer? If you would lead God's people, learn to sanctify silence. Learn to saturate solitude with God's presence. Emmanuel, God with us.

Pastoral ministry has been, for many including this writer, one of the loneliest places. Having been on a mountain alone, between God and men, I can say it is a source of lifelong strength for the practicing pastor. Joshua's experience here isn't told to us. But God never wastes time—it wasn't an accident that Joshua found himself here alone. We can all benefit from such solitary times with God. You don't really need a mountain, of course. It's not really the place that's important.

chapter twenty

WHAT KIND OF NOISE ARE WE MAKING?

On the way down the mountain, Moses and Joshua heard a noise. Joshua the warrior said, "*...There is a noise of war in the camp*" (Exodus 32:17). He was already holding his sword handle in its scabbard. Joshua was set to run down the mountain with a war cry on his lips. However, the older Moses listened longer, closer, and analyzed: "*...It is not the noise of the shout of victory, Nor the noise of the cry of defeat, But the sound of singing...*" (Exodus 32:18)! He was right. They were worshipping an idol. They were heard halfway down a mountain. But the idol made a bigger impression than their worship. Now, what would you have done? What would have happened today?

Of course, even false worship in the modern world wouldn't involve a golden calf. It wouldn't be so obviously idolatrous. Yet many things we do in church wouldn't stand Moses's analysis. Is our worship... the shout of victory? Sometimes it is, in a good way. Is our worship the cry of defeat? Far too often this is the subject matter of modern worship songs... the cry of yet another bad day of defeat. The desperate cry for a parental hug... from God Almighty.

Then again, is our worship no more than "the noise of singing?" Oh, dear would-be pastor, can you discern when worship has deteriorated to mere noise?! The pastor or leader of God's work must learn by looking at his own worship—search for reality in our own worship; leaders must understand what pleases God and sense the lack of it in the noise.

Analysis isn't common anymore. Yet the man of God, the elder, the pastor, must learn to discern truth from error. The starting place is your own heart. Moses taught Joshua something that day. Don't judge until you're close enough to see and hear well. True worship involves the audible and the visual, the sound of singing and the direction of affection. These can declare truth or error. Also, Moses demonstrated a mature response to the failure of God's people in worship. Before he spoke, Moses dealt with the focus of their false worship. Moses, with righteous rage, destroyed the golden calf, burning the gold to useless powder. His judgement on falsehood in worship was instant and decisive. This is the clear-headed thinking of the man of God even when he is angry. Joshua was watching.

Is this Moses getting angry with Israel again? Maybe. But we share his frustration at this moment. He should have heard singing of a different sort. Israel couldn't wait for a few weeks for Moses to return. Having addressed Aaron's failure, he turned to the people. His words are powerful and have been used to challenge both sinner and saint throughout the ages: "... *Whoever is on the Lord's side—come to me*" (Exodus 32:26)! Hymns have been written and sung with these words ringing in the hearts of God's people. Many a sinner has stepped over to the Lord's side under the influence of God's Word and the invitation of the famous hymn by Frances Ridley Havargal, "Who is on the Lord's Side?" Joshua stood with Moses as he spoke—where would you have been standing if you had been there? If you don't know... you should decide now! The pastor must clearly know where he stands on many issues. Certainly, where he stands on worship.

The would-be pastor must understand worship. Today we have no guidelines, no rules or patterns to follow, and many don't care. Worship is questionable as it is practiced today. We are happy to let go of many of the old hymns, happier still to be rid of hymn books and projectors. But perhaps not so comfortable with actual worship. It isn't for us to judge in our small country congregation. But we shouldn't simply emulate the worship of others. God doesn't want secondhand copies, and certainly no acting. Be yourself when you worship God!

What Kind of Noise Are We Making?

Worship first in the presence of God and with an open Bible. Then carry that studied experience to your congregation. Also, remember you aren't Moses, and they aren't Israel. True worship need not be quiet; it should be intergenerational; it should be holy. Of course, worship is essentially a matter of the heart. It always begins with my heart! But there are other governing factors than just me and my heart. Joshua understood these nuances.

chapter twenty-one

BEING UNABLE TO STAND

The book of Exodus finishes with the details, rules, and designs required for Israel's life. It finishes after the Tabernacle had been built. During these chapters, the narrative is about Moses. Joshua is always there in the background. At all the significant moments from the Exodus to his death, Joshua is with Moses, one of history's greatest men. He takes it all in. He learns and grows through these long events. This was God's college for Joshua. We must recognize that in our years of preparation for serving the Lord, much of the time will be in the background. We may want to be in the forefront, but the Lord may hold us back. Exodus finishes with the glory of God so filling the Temple that Moses can't stand to minister. This is an awesome aim, at least in the heart, of every man called of God.

God filling His church with His presence is so powerful an experience that you must stop speaking, stop ministering, sit down with the people and let God be God. We have moved from one man with God in a solitary place to a full church being unable to stand or sing—such is the presence of God! Learn to discover both if you can.

This isn't just a model for pastors today. This is the word of God! Would you sense His presence? Are you brave enough to sit down and give God your pulpit? To say His words, to make Him the centre of your pulpit? To hide and remain hidden? Not to mention yourself in His presence... not even to thank Him for His help in your diligent study or prayerful preparation or your lack of fitness for the occasion, which is all still about you? It's about you trying to hide behind the cross. Just hide! Just *don't talk about yourself at all!* Let Him increase while you decrease. These moments require personal diligence to ensure that the Glory of God fills the temple. *Don't imagine that you won't be tempted to turn the pulpit into a stage. Never imagine that the pulpit is free from temptation.* The devil wants to dislodge, to discolour, to destroy, or, just ever so slightly, to spoil the pulpit.

Joshua was listening. Joshua was watching. He had a lot of learning to do before he led God's people into their Promised Land. He was happy to remain Moses's assistant. He was clearly not ambitious, not grasping, not proud. He was already a warrior. A warrior in training to be a statesman, but above all, he was a real man, refined in the presence of God. Are you?

chapter twenty-two

BEING A CHOICE MAN

We read some accounts of Joshua in the book of Numbers. A situation arises. Two men prophesied in the camp, and they were reported to Moses in Joshua's hearing. Joshua is introduced to the reader as "...*Joshua the son of Nun, Moses' assistant, one of his choice men...*" (Num 11:28). Here, the scriptures show a maturing in Joshua, having risen in Moses's estimation. He is 'a man of choice.' This is a testimony to the benefit of steady, diligent learning and growing as a man while being a mere assistant.

There is no substitute for the maturing of time to develop a man of God. Knowledge and daily practice are factors that improve and develop us, moulding the inner man. Inspired scripture leaves Joshua out of the narrative for a time until this growth is evident. Now, he is recognized as being 'choice.'

This growth in Joshua wasn't a product of complacently doing nothing. He may not be on the front line or noticed by anyone but God. But secretly, quietly, Joshua was waiting on God. The diligent servant is alert to His master's needs, willing to rise to the occasion. If not called upon, he waits!

We have already noted that Joshua is a listener. He is also an observer, alert to life around him. The waiting is when the lessons, mulled over and learned, take root in the heart and mind. Waiting morphs the lessons into the man. Naturally, lessons reinforced over time become part of who a believer is as a person. This is what is intended by the title of the book *Being Joshua*. So, back to the incident where Joshua is described...

This 'choice' servant gets it wrong again and is mercilessly exposed by Moses. Joshua insists that Moses forbid these two men to prophesy. Moses recognized what Joshua was thinking, seeing his motivation without an explanation. Joshua was protecting his master. Moses didn't need protection. Hear one lesson Joshua learns: "... *Oh that all the Lord's people were prophets and that the Lord would put His Spirit upon them*" (Num. 11:29). Joshua was content with one man anointed by God's Spirit... Moses was not. God is not.

How easy it is to be content, to even feel blessed with one good man in your congregation, such as the pastor or an elder, or even yourself. Moses bleeds at such a stinted vision. God sent His Spirit on all of those gathered at Pentecost. 120 believers were in one place with one accord. What is your vision for your church? Or the church you imagine serving in? Is it a wealthy congregation? A middle-class congregation? Perhaps a musically gifted or financially secure congregation? Or is it a congregation where the Lord has put His Spirit upon all of them?!

The Lord wants to fill all His people with the Holy Spirit. Pray that you will not be the one to resist Him or them. Pray that the Lord will make you the example by which to make them hungry for God's Spirit. This book isn't a Pentecostal sermon! This is the heart of Old Testament Moses. Indeed, the heart of God Himself. Joshua was given a fundamental lesson about the nature of the people of God. Leaders don't have more of the Spirit than members simply on account of their office. They require a greater diligence in maintaining what God has given them due to their office. But God is willing to fill all who seek Him with His Holy Spirit.

Moses wisely says, "...*Are you zealous for my sake?*" (Numbers 11:29). The implication is... "don't be!" Remember also that God looks out for the integrity of His servants and their position. And the word 'elder' or 'overseer' isn't the position of an office. It is essentially a type of person. A person who is recognized as a mature believer and naturally watches out for the people of God. An elder is merely being 'recognized' for who he is when he is called an elder. We can appoint deacons, tell them what we want them to do, and tell them to do it. We can ask people to fulfill tasks, but we can't make someone an elder—the person must represent the biblical example. We can help the man who has these elements to improve, but we can't make him what he isn't.

These are lessons for Joshua then and for us today. Above all, don't be afraid of God demonstrating His power through another person in the congregation. Do not be afraid for the pastor or yourself as the pastor. Never view the blessings of others as a threat to yourself. Be the rare kind of pastor who would gladly step aside without any sense of loss and make way for another's gifting to operate as God leads you. That mentality will keep you alert and humble. God deliver us from striving to keep our job while losing our calling. These principles apply to every believer in their Christian life.

SECTION VI:
INAUGURATION

chapter twenty-three
PEOPLE BEING FICKLE

Numbers 13:16

Joshua is chosen to be one of the spies sent into Canaan to spy out the land (Num 13:16). There were twelve spies. The children's hymn sums the story up well "Twelve men went to spy in Canaan, ten were bad, two were good! ... Some saw giants big and tall, some the grapes in clusters fall..." Joshua and Caleb were the two good spies. They were very positive. We are told these days to always be positive. Positivity is seen as the key that opens every door. Well... not in this instance... The response of the people was to want to stone Joshua and Caleb for their 'positive' report (Num 14:10).

Joshua demonstrated the strength required to lead God's people, to say what is right and to stand by it, even when his job and life were threatened. Joshua was still listening... still watching! He would remember these moments. We must apply these principles in our lives.

In Scotland, we say, "People are fickle." That means unpredictable, changeable, and difficult. We will be in trouble if we don't understand this. Group mentality is a real thing. There are individuals who influence the group. Often, they don't even realize they are doing it. Others do so deliberately. Joshua did the right thing, the spiritual thing, the believing thing. But the people weren't happy. It's important to keep expectations realistic. This is the moment when the Lord tells everyone that only Joshua and Caleb will enter Canaan because of their good report. The people will die in the wilderness.

The next generation will go into Canaan. Our responses, words, and actions carry consequences.

In Numbers 27, there is a major development in the story of Joshua. Moses asked the Lord to choose a man to lead Israel in battle and be their guide and leader.

> *And the Lord said to Moses: "Take Joshua the son of Nun with you, a man in whom is the Spirit, and lay your hand on him; set him before Eleazar the priest and before all the congregation, and inaugurate him in their sight. And you shall give some of your authority to him, that all the congregation of the children of Israel may be obedient..."*
> —Numbers 27:18-21

What a moment this is for Joshua. The Lord describes Joshua as a man *in whom is the Spirit* of God. Surely this is awesome proof that God prepares men throughout life's issues for His service. When the time is right, He calls them. God wants Joshua to serve, and Joshua is willing and ready to serve. This is what God had been preparing Joshua for, this harmony of God's timing and Joshua's preparation.

chapter twenty-four
BEING INAUGURATED

There is a 'ceremony' and there is a 'moment.' *We can do without ceremony; we cannot miss the moment.* It is a ceremony that recognizes God's call on Joshua and inaugurates him to the role he will fulfill. The whole congregation takes part as witnesses. The religious leaders invoke the presence of God and acknowledge His approval. Joshua's responsibilities are defined to some degree. That's the ceremony (with variations).

This ceremony celebrates a wonderful moment for the man called of God. It carries an awesome and heavy sense of both privilege and responsibility. It should fill the ordinand, that is what we call him, with a sense of awe. Because God's people have expressed this recognition of him publicly. He should be filled with encouragement. He should feel compelled, energized. He should feel prepared and ready. He may feel it has taken a long time to arrive! He should feel he has been let loose like Lazarus: "… *Loose him and let him go*" (John 11:44). In a day soon to come, they may well attempt to bind him again, but that is a sermon for the congregation! This man was so prepared and so recognized that he should be unstoppable for some considerable time. But right now, as it were, Joshua can't just get on with it. Still to come is this 'moment.' This instance, performed by Moses, is simply described as "He (Moses) laid his hands upon him" (Numbers 27:23).

Moses laid his hands on Joshua and passed on the leadership mantle. It was a brief, unsung, simple act; not magical, but yet a powerful, spiritual moment. Moses had no power to transfer anything physically or spiritually. But the idea of laying on of hands has been recognized in multiple ways down the centuries among the people of God. It is seen to be an act of significance. Not so much that it "does" something significant but that is "is" something significant. It isn't presented as extreme as some religious groups imagine. Nor is it a cold, empty tradition after generations of abuse. Moses is passing on the leadership of God's people. God laid that on Moses and Moses laid it on Joshua. This was a special occasion that conveyed a selection and responsibility. Moses brought them out, and Joshua would take them in!

God approves of this, and it is witnessed by people. The candidate isn't magically changed by this event. This is a moment of recognizing credentials obtained through life, as opposed to a moment creating something. But still, the person will be different. Like Joseph being seventeen, Joshua was as he should be at this time, ready. Since the ceremony itself receives the approval of God, it will influence all of those involved in a life-changing way.

Sometimes we think the Spirit of God is only present after Pentecost. Nothing could be further from the truth. Here in the Old Testament, we find God the Holy Spirit evident in the life of God's people. This moment was a spiritual moment where God's presence was felt. Do we need to expand it into a rich theatrical event? It doesn't need to be defined; it needs to be experienced. Do we need a fresh set of words? A new outfit or symbols, hangings, songs and chants? Is there a need for any human interference at all? No. But we love to take these simple moments and complicate them; often the church has unnecessarily exaggerated their legitimate purpose because God's presence is absent! We feel a need to fill the moment with 'something.' But His presence is all we need. If we lack it, nothing can replace it.

The need is closer to home than the clerical robe maker. The pastor must see this pertinently and do all in his power to resist anything created to replace God's presence. It's an Old Testament text. So of course, there is ceremony. The Old Testament illustrates a reality that is yet to come. Christ has still to be born. Pentecost is a long time away; the scriptures have not been given. Yet... the text describing this ceremony is simple and brief. It says, "*Moses laid his hands upon him and inaugurated him*". Now understand that despite the lack of a big religious moment, Joshua could not but be affected. It would humble, strengthen, encourage, and challenge him for the rest of his days. Men seem to love ceremony. But it is this 'moment,' God's presence, which makes it real.

The time between the ceremony and the real work God calls us to may vary. But Joshua has a day ahead when he will require all the help he can muster to lead these people. So, too, with the pastor. You need the recognition of the whole church to be able to do the job. Self-appointed pastors are on an uphill climb; many would say they aren't legitimate at all. The ministry isn't a self-appointed position. Nor is it all about the individual. It's about God's church.

This is too serious a place for ecclesiastical extravagance. Neither is it a place for primitive reductionism. Central to this moment, in this narrative, is the belief in the person and work of the Holy Spirit, and a people who hear God when He speaks. Joshua the candidate was passive. He had not been passive up until now. He will not be passive for the rest of his life. This was God's moment.

chapter twenty-five

BEING ENCOURAGED

In Deuteronomy 1:38 the people were exhorted to encourage Joshua. While the best encouragement comes directly from the Word of God, learn to accept encouragement from anyone. We often think encouragement should flow from the greater to the lesser. Yet here a stubborn and disobedient people are the ones God commands to encourage Joshua.

Pastors who can't take spoken encouragement from lesser saints have inverted God's order. The Lord will even send the unbeliever to bring you encouragement when the church fails you. Don't be looking to the important people who make you feel important. Look to the flock of God over which he made you an overseer. They were commanded to encourage Joshua. You want to be a leader? A pastor? Then begin by encouraging your pastor now, in prayer.

This encourager doesn't even have to speak. Encouragement isn't necessarily verbal. Your humble, obedient walk with God encourages those who know you, particularly your pastor.

The smile on their face speaks encouragement. Our entire demeanour can be uplifting. The stories that run round the congregation, of your humble self-effacing acts of kindness, and your faithful witnessing, these are among the best forms of encouragement.

chapter twenty-six

BEING WATCHED

Deuteronomy 3:21

In these early chapters of Deuteronomy, we are told about Israel's wilderness battles. Two kings are of note because they seem to have been well known. They are Sihon king of Heshbon, and Og king of Bashan. Israel defeats them. Great, powerful kingdoms are falling before Israel. God defeated their enemies in the wilderness, and Joshua is taking it all in.... Canaan and all its inhabitants are now also watching and concerned.

They don't like what they hear. They are being told remarkable stories about Israel's God and His power to save. Rahab is listening to quiet conversations in her establishment. Was business on a downturn? Fear restrains men's passions. She kept hearing whispers... Jehovah, Bashan, Og, Israel. Maybe even Joshua, but certainly she heard the name 'Moses the man of God.' Joshua doesn't know this anguish is building in Canaan's great cities. We never know all that God is doing for us until after the event, maybe not until heaven.

In Deuteronomy 31:3, Moses tells them Joshua will go over before them and they shall take Canaan. Then, in Deuteronomy 31:7, Moses speaks to Joshua in the sight of the people. He tells him to have courage. He then says to Joshua *"And the Lord, He is the One who goes before you. He will be with you, He will not leave you nor forsake you; do not fear nor be dismayed"* (Deut. 31:8). God will lead Joshua, as Joshua leads the people. Joshua goes first. Here is a basic principle for a pastor.

We don't lead from behind or send people to work for the Lord. We go, they follow. We aren't talking about any specific area of God's work but about the principle of leading by example. Pastors who sit in their comfortable offices studying may produce real, serious sermons, or perhaps not. But if the pastor can't give his testimony at a street meeting, he will have difficulty getting his congregation to give their testimony in a church service… (Does anybody do that these days? We should!). Joshua had to go over before the people. Pastor, you must be at the front, leading.

chapter twenty-seven
BEING MOSES'S SUCCESSOR

Deuteronomy 31:14–15

We now have the second inauguration of Joshua into a position of leadership. This time, to replace Moses. What a thought! Moses is going to die. Joshua must replace him. Perhaps you imagine yourself taking charge of a large church. Consider this situation carefully. In many cases, you are setting yourself up to fail! You are a beginner. The previous pastor/leader was a lifelong and presumably a successful person. Will you cope with the myriad of potential problems as soon as the honeymoon period is over? Comparisons will be made, it is inevitable. Better to start with a normal-sized charge, than to aim too high. This may seem too practical a comment. The guidance pastors must give must mix the practical realities of life with the eternal theological principles of the Bible. But don't misunderstand, "... *If God is for us, who can be against us?*" (Rom 8:31). No difficulty or problem is too great for Him, but lots of them are too big for us. Be prepared to do the small things and gradually grow into the bigger things in the providence of God.

Now, if God is with you like He was with Joshua, you will be ok... you really will. The people who loved Moses also accepted Joshua. But observe that Israel to this day hasn't been able to let Moses rest in peace and accept Jesus who in every sense replaced him.

The Lord appeared at Joshua's inauguration! God certainly owned this moment in front of all the people. Joshua was getting the same authentication as Moses. God's presence in your ministry will expunge any other presence.

In Deuteronomy, we read these words: *"Then He inaugurated Joshua the son of Nun, and said, 'Be strong and of good courage; for you shall bring the children of Israel into the land of which I swore to them, and I will be with you'"* (31:23). Now by this stage in Joshua's story, you must have noticed that these words are used repeatedly. I will take the liberty then of repeating what can't be said enough… encourage one another, encourage your pastor, encourage your wife, husband, children. Encourage your church. The list is endless. Encouragement is never finished; it is a constant necessity in the Christian walk. Above all, encourage yourself in the Lord daily. That is a faith exercise. If you need encouragement, read your Bible! It has been sufficient encouragement for the church through the centuries.

The last reference to Joshua in Deuteronomy says, *"Now Joshua the son of Nun was full of the spirit of wisdom, for Moses had laid his hands on him; so the children of Israel heeded him, and did as the Lord had commanded Moses"* (Deuteronomy 34:9). Two things to note here. First, Joshua is now full of the Spirit and wisdom. There is very little wisdom in youth unless it was planted there by a senior. Wisdom is a mature characteristic. It is produced in life's noise and in life's quietness. But it is essential for all areas of church leadership. Joshua had attained wisdom.

The second thing is what the text says regarding Moses… Joshua was full of the Spirit because Moses had laid his hands upon him. Here we see a double truth: Moses imparted wisdom to Joshua every day, but in the event of laying on of his hands he also imparted a spiritual wisdom—wisdom that the Bible tells us can only come from above. James 3:17 says *"But the wisdom that is from above…"* This is a spiritual wisdom from God. It was conveyed via Moses to Joshua. This wasn't a religious rite of passage or mere tradition. This was a unique need being met.

SECTION VII:
THEREFORE ARISE AFTER MOSES

chapter twenty-eight
AFTER THE DEATH OF MOSES

Joshua 1

After the death of Moses the servant of the Lord, it came to pass that the Lord spoke to Joshua the son of Nun, Moses' assistant, saying..."
—Joshua 1:1

The book of Joshua follows naturally from Deuteronomy with the death of Moses, the servant of the Lord. The scripture sets the scene for what follows.

What do we do when our leader dies? We must *"...arise, go over this Jordan..."* (Joshua 1:2), whatever 'this Jordan' looks like. We must read the words of these verses and transfer them to our circumstances. The Old Testament was written for every generation. Believers must revere the past by reading God's dealings with His people and seeing ourselves there. He has never changed, and neither have we! Joshua had to face the implications of Moses's death. We must face up to every situation of loss or change. God has something to say to us in such circumstances. He spoke to Joshua at the death of Moses. He is speaking there to us.

A freshly filled grave can feel like the emptiest place on earth. For at least forty years, Joshua's existence had been filled by Moses. Yet after a brief time of mourning, Joshua seems to have been able to respond to the Lord when He spoke. There is no evidence of a struggle though it couldn't have been easy. He is announced early as *"Joshua the son of Nun..."* Then, so we don't think the past is irrelevant, he is also identified as *"Moses's assistant."*

Many of us see the Lord through another person. When they die, a cold gap appears in our life. This is real grief. It carries all the symptoms of the loss of a family member or maybe more. There is nothing wrong with appreciating godly influences. We can even learn and grow under bad influences if we choose. However, when these relationships come to an end, we must rise and grasp life with our whole being. The runner's 'baton' is now ours to carry. If you drop it, pick it up quickly and get in the race again. Remember, you will have to pass on your 'baton' to someone else, maybe more than once in your life. Make sure you pass it on well. Make it super easy for them to take it from you. Remember to let it go.

Joshua and the whole nation revered Moses. They continue to regard Moses as their chief statesman to this day. But for the Lord, Joshua, and Israel... *"Moses My servant is dead..."* (Joshua 1:2).

There is often a brief timelessness between leaders. This isn't a vacuum. It is a holy moment that silently resets everything before God speaks. Moses would always be in Joshua's thoughts and affection. But Joshua realized that there was no time to hang on. He had to let Moses die and start listening in the empty space for God. Sometimes we want to keep things alive that should be buried. We stand with heads bowed in respect for our loved one, and God's Spirit gently calls us to look up and away. Sometimes God is waiting to interject a 'promised land' into our sadness. He is waiting for our Moses to peacefully die inside us. Often a void must be felt that produces realization before the Lord speaks. Only then does He have our complete attention. So, Moses is dead—what happens now? God speaks to Joshua the son of Nun, Moses's minister.

God acknowledges Joshua's rise to becoming "Moses's Assistant." Joshua earned that title. But to the Lord, Joshua was more importantly *Joshua the son of Nun*—an ordinary child of God—just like you and I. It's who God is that matters. God is behind the believer's experiences in life. Joshua is taken out of his empty space into the very presence of God. And so, the Bible says, *"After the*

After the Death of Moses

death of Moses… the Lord spoke to Joshua the Son of Nun…" (Joshua 1:1). Without Moses, Joshua becomes ordinary again, yet conversely, he isn't ordinary, he is a child of God. And God speaks to Him.

The pastor in this situation may feel alone now that his strongest support has gone. He should remember this moment because Joshua wasn't alone. He isn't even weaker. God is with him as He was with Moses. Leaders must learn this clearly and grasp it by faith in a time of difficulty. *"As I was with Moses, so I will be with you …"* (Joshua 1:5). Hear the echo of the burning bush: *"I am"* (Exodus 3:14)! That is, *"I am always who I am."* Regardless of the circumstances, God is unchangeable.

chapter twenty-nine

THEREFORE ARISE

"Moses My servant is dead. Now therefore, arise, go over this Jordan, you and all this people, to the land which I am giving to them—the children of Israel."
—Joshua 1:2

What does God say to Joshua? He says, "arise!" This word paints a picture. Had they collapsed in grief or become dormant? To arise requires energy. Joshua wasn't the only child of God to have been commanded to "arise." *"Arise, shine; for your light has come...the glory of the Lord is risen upon you"* (Isaiah 60:1). The prophet Isaiah called God's people to stand up after a period of stagnation. Even God is described in this text as having "risen." Joshua must also arise. This isn't just an internal change of attitude. It results in movement.

Often the man or woman of God isn't where they should be in their calling. *"Go over this Jordan" "Go into the whole world..."* (Mark 16:15). When God sees a willingness to serve, even reluctantly, He will accept you where you are, but He won't leave you there. He "calls" us where He wants us to be. Joshua is willing and arises to the task—in terms that consider his own frailty and limitations. The Lord will help him.

The obstacle of the river is diminished by the Lord's choice of words, *"This Jordan."* God revealed to Joshua how He saw the Jordan River. For Joshua, it's a big problem. However, the Lord poured derision on it: "this Jordan." God doesn't always take our difficulties away. He sometimes walks us through them and will do the same for all who respond in faith. Joshua grasped this, and when he spoke to the people, his strength was visible.

chapter thirty

BEING MORE THAN YOURSELF

But there is more revealed in these early verses for us to ponder. Since the mid-20th century, we have lived under the curse of individualism, a concept that has withered us and resulted in wasted lives over selfish decades. For the believer, life is never 'just about me.' The greatest commandment includes loving our neighbour. To Joshua the word of God is, *"Arise and go over this Jordan, you and all this people…"* (Joshua 1:2). Never allow yourself to think your life is just about yourself. Your faith will impact others. Indeed, the land which Joshua must go up and possess is for these very people. Joshua will only have a short time in the Promised Land before he dies too. The nation of Israel is still there today.

So, the Lord's servants must encourage themselves with this understanding even if it seems toilsome and thankless. The people will also cross this Jordan. The place God brings you into. Imagine Joshua in old age looking out over Canaan. Happy families rejoicing in the land filled with milk and honey. I imagine when the land was settled and Joshua walked into town, they cheered and wept for gratitude. They loved him and appreciated him. He shared with them what God gave them under his influence. God's servants share God's spiritual blessings with those to whom they minister.

The man or woman who would serve God must always be thinking and praying for others. The Lord's Prayer illustrates this quietly but thoroughly, *"Our Father,"* *"Our Daily bread,"* *"Our Sins,"* *"Others"* (Matt 6:9–13, see my next book). Self permeates everything in our thinking today. The individual is just part of the whole, be it a family, or a community, or a church, or a nation. We think about one without thinking about the other. The servant of God must overcome this small-minded, solitary obsession. Be like Jesus. Paul writing to the Philippians says, *"Let nothing be done through selfish ambition or conceit, but in lowliness of mind let each esteem others better than himself. Let each of you look out not only for his own interests, but also for the interests of others"* (Phil. 2:2–4). This is the man of God. This is Joshua and all the people! If you would serve God, it must be you too.

SECTION VIII:
COMPELLED AND CONTROLLED

chapter thirty-one

JOSHUA'S FAITH

"Every place that the sole of your foot will tread upon I have given you, as I said to Moses."
—Joshua 1:3

Well, although this walk of faith isn't easy, it's strangely simple. *"Every place that the sole of your foot shall tread... I have given you."* The Lord tells Joshua how he will overcome the land—walk on it! Just keep walking on it. Don't stop. Keep putting one foot in front of the other... by faith. Believe God is with you... as He was with Moses. This practice of daily faith produces the unique quality of perseverance. A real sign of a real believer. The potential leader must have learned to finish what he starts before he enters service in God's church.

Faith is built on something God has already finished. Note that the text is past tense. *"I have given you..."* For the Lord, the fight was already won. Joshua believed God had already done it! What a different man or woman you'd be if such faith entered your heart. The believer is only as strong as his walk of faith.

While Joshua's future was secure, he wasn't over-confident or arrogant. *Faith is a beautiful, energetic, and strong, dependency.* It is visible to onlookers. It evokes envy. Faith confuses the unbeliever yet fills him with a deep search of heart. In real uncertainty, believers appear to have an unbelievable calm! They are often very ordinary people, yet the faith they express reveals God in action. It is essential that believers express this faith confidently and without arrogance.

chapter thirty-two

FAITH LARGE, BUT LIMITED

"From the wilderness and this Lebanon as far as the great river, the River Euphrates, all the land of the Hittites, and to the Great Sea toward the going down of the sun, shall be your territory."

—Joshua 1:4

Joshua's faith is limited to believing only what God promised. *God did not promise Abraham an empire*, just a land with boundaries. Israel's neighbours then and now had nothing to fear. There would be no unlimited 'expansionism.' They would accept the limits set in God's promise. Some think that faith is weak if it is limited. Yet also note that the limits of this faith for Joshua are set very large. Faith isn't a free-for-all. Faith is controlled by obedience and its limits are set by the Lord. Faith is simultaneously compelled and controlled by God. Here Joshua has been promised the land of Canaan, a sizeable promise yet limited.

Also, this challenge to Joshua's faith isn't a lifetime exercise. It's a limited challenge. The exercise of faith that is unlimited is that which believes for eternal salvation in Christ. It includes all the eternal promises of the gospel. That faith is unlimited, unrestrained, and out of this world!

chapter thirty-three

FAITH HAS ENEMIES

No man shall be able to stand before you all the days of your life; as I was with Moses, so I will be with you. I will not leave you nor forsake you. Be strong and of good courage, for to this people you shall divide as an inheritance the land which I swore to their fathers to give them.
—Joshua 1: 5–6

This promise is for "...*all the days of your life.*" Joshua wouldn't be fighting all his life. The battles of faith are less than the help promised. The promise is always there for Joshua even when there's no threat of war. Perhaps he heard of wars and rumours of wars. Like today, these wars often didn't come to anything. But for children and adults, when threats disturb our peace, God's promises are there like the structure of a house—every time they are needed and lots of times when they don't appear to be needed, they remain solidly in place.

Imagine Joshua feeling the strain, feeling insufficient for the task. Imagine him under criticism, being compared to Moses. He wouldn't instantly feel like Moses! In these moments, the word of God encourages him... *As I was With Moses, so shall I be with you!* The Lord promises Joshua that he will fulfill the promise given to Moses. Joshua believed this word.

Only be strong and very courageous, that you may observe to do according to all the law which Moses My servant

commanded you; do not turn from it to the right hand or to the left, that you may prosper wherever you go.
—Joshua 1:7

This tells us that faith is saturated by the word of God. This promise points to its source as God. Faith and God's Word go together. When we read, meditate, and study it, it strengthens our faith. The man who reads God's Word will be strong in faith.

Words can be full of life and vitality, substantial, life-changing. Words of faith rise to the level of glorifying God. Our words of faith shouldn't be proudful or about us, they should glorify God. Faith is our conversation. It influences our verbal responses and discussions. It should never depart from our mouths. Faith, then, isn't only a silent substructure. It isn't just the hidden anchor of the believer. Faith is to be expressed verbally and publicly.

chapter thirty-four

FAITH WITH HEART AND OBEDIENCE

"...Observe to do according to all the law..."
—Joshua 1:7

*F*aith uncoupled from obedience has only a thin, brittle surface. It has no depth. Like a brittle shell, it shatters with a sharp blow. Faith separated from obedience can be shocked straight back into unbelief. Onlookers are often surprised at the instant fall of such individuals. Obedience strengthens faith.

> *This Book of the Law shall not depart from your mouth, but you shall meditate in it day and night, that you may observe to do according to all that is written in it. For then you will make your way prosperous, and then you will have good success.*
> —Joshua 1:8

Faith must be in tandem with God's Word. How many hopeless fantasies have been laid on the people of God? Often leaders covet miraculous interventions to ratify themselves as special, or to make themselves rich. How much fake faith has been demanded of sick believers, condemned for their lack of this 'faith.' Those who make such large claims for others don't know the word of God.

Years of church life can be wasted... yes, wasted on entire fictions pushed by deluded leaders. We all get it wrong sometimes. But when 'faith' is demanded on the word of the 'pastor,' warning bells should sound. When the outcome of the faith calls for a grand reputation, or worse, a mansion for the pastor, onlookers are right to see the folly.

True faith produces prosperity and success for the believer. Prosperity, for the Christian, isn't necessarily expressed by finances or power. It can be, but more often it is a solid character and a good reputation. The achievements of Joshua's faith glorified God.

SECTION IX:
JOSHUA STEPS UP

chapter thirty-five

THE BIG PICTURE

Have I not commanded you? Be strong and of good courage; do not be afraid, nor be dismayed, for the Lord your God is with you wherever you go"
—Joshua 1:9

Do not be afraid or discouraged. Yes, Joshua was a warrior, a man of faith and obedience. Yet he also needed encouragement. How often do we look upon leaders and think they don't feel fear or discouragement? Yet Elijah was "... *a man with a nature like ours...*" (James 5:17).

Please see, however, that this courage isn't based inside us—God stays with us in our daily walk. He has given us His Spirit. The text says, "... *nor be dismayed, for the Lord your God is with you wherever you go*" (Joshua 1:9).

The presence of God with us is so important for our walk in this world. *The presence of God is our confidence.* How could we be afraid of any man, any situation, or any danger? Yet, while we shouldn't fear, remember the psalmist says, "*Whenever I am afraid, I will trust in You*" (Psalm 56:3). We are human.

"*Then Joshua commanded the officers of the people, saying...*" (Joshua 1:10). What effect did this have on Joshua? He stepped up to the task "*Joshua commanded the officers...*" Now, this is Joshua having left Moses and what Moses represented. He didn't insist upon mourning. That time had passed. He rejected the fear. God knows everything that is going to happen! Now is the time to step up, get up, and go!

"Pass through the host, and command the people, saying, 'Prepare provisions for yourselves, for within three days you will cross over this Jordan, to go in to possess the land, which the Lord your God is giving you to possess'" (Joshua 1:11).

It's an awesome statement, simple and concise. The officers and the people understood fully what was happening. He tells them to prepare. This summarizes the instructions given to every child of God when they come to faith in Christ... prepare for a journey to inherit the promised land! Do you see life in such terms? If you don't, you are missing out on a world of inspiration to live fully for God and for your neighbour.

chapter thirty-six

THE SMALL DETAIL

"And to the Reubenites, the Gadites, and half the tribe of Manasseh Joshua spoke..."
—Joshua 1:12–14

Moses allowed these tribes to settle in the land before Jordan. Moses allowed this on the condition that they would still go across and fight until the people of God were settled in Canaan. This is interesting because it was an immediate potential threat to the whole project. Joshua could have had an uprising from the people refusing to cross Jordan.

The significance of this would be the heathen saying God had failed. Israel's failure would be blamed on God. Moses had expressed this when he pleaded with the Lord not to destroy Israel at the incident of the golden calf. Exodus tells us: *"... Why should the Egyptians speak, and say, 'He brought them out to harm them, to kill them in the mountains, and to consume them from the face of the earth'?"* (Exodus 32:12). So often, we only see ourselves hurting from our failures; when a greater injustice goes unnoticed against the Lord, the heathen criticizes our God!

At the outset, Joshua recognized an arrangement, perhaps forgotten, that could potentially wreck the enterprise. This showed great ability to see details while looking at the big picture. We all need this skill. Joshua reminded them of what Moses commanded, adding authority to his recent role, *"Remember the word which Moses the servant of the Lord commanded you, saying, 'The Lord your God is giving you rest and is giving you this land'"* (Joshua 1:13).

Joshua also reminded them, *"Your wives, your little ones, and your livestock shall remain in the land which Moses gave you on this side of the Jordan. But you shall pass before your brethren armed, all your mighty men of valour, and help them"* (Joshua 1:14).

Joshua didn't take it for granted that they would remember the details. He spelled it out fully. Adhering to these details was essential to possess the Promised Land. God attends to detail.

> *until the Lord has given your brethren rest, as He gave you, and they also have taken possession of the land which the Lord your God is giving them. Then you shall return to the land of your possession and enjoy it, which Moses the Lord's servant gave you on this side of the Jordan toward the sunrise.*
>
> —Joshua 1:15

The men from these tribes couldn't enter into their rest until their brethren crossed over and conquered Canaan. The people accepted this and stood in solidarity with the two-and-a-half tribes. Remember this moment because it would be doubted later and bring these honourable tribes into danger and Israel into division. This was due to a greater enemy than armies... gossip!

"So they answered Joshua, saying, 'All that you command us we will do, and wherever you send us we will go'" (Joshua 1:16).

Observe the unity and enthusiasm of Israel. Remember, they recently lost Moses, and they have a new leader. When they were immediately confronted with the Jordan, they committed themselves to Joshua. *All that you command and wherever you send us...* that is thorough obedience. Sometimes obedience must be expressed vocally and publicly.

We need to renew this kind of statement before God regularly. At this moment they were beautifully and convincingly giving themselves to Joshua and to the Lord. This is the new generation, whose fathers failed. It seems that they have learned from their fathers' mistakes; God grant that our children will learn from ours.

chapter thirty-seven
UNITY IN MUTUAL EXHORTATION

"Just as we heeded Moses in all things, so we will heed you. Only the Lord your God be with you, as He was with Moses."
—Joshua 1:17

Israel was determined to be obedient. But they hadn't been obedient to Moses *in all things*! Often our memory fails concerning the past. God understands us. Leaders must also understand this, having recognized it in themselves.

They also wanted God to be with Joshua, and they expressed to what extent: *"...as He was with Moses."* God doesn't set the church up to function then leave it to itself! God sent the Holy Spirit to guide and keep the church in all things. Nevertheless, *'God be with you as He was with Moses'* is an awesome benediction.

"Whoever rebels against your command and does not heed your words, in all that you command him, shall be put to death. Only be strong and of good courage" (Joshua 1:18).

Now here we have a cutting edge added to these beautiful words of commitment. Those who disobey Joshua will be put to death. The people appear very thoughtful here. They keep returning to the need for Joshua himself to be right, not just the people themselves. How often leaders and people blame each other. Israel, after forty years wandering in the desert as a result of disobedience, is intent that both they and their leader be obedient: *"Only be strong and of good courage."* This is a good start to Canaan.

We know the atmosphere illustrated here. The church is optimistic, totally committed, and generally unified around one big challenge. It is an awesome thing to be a part of this kind of church. However, the energy level needed to maintain this atmosphere is often unrealistically high. Sometimes the pastor or the prayerful member senses an uneasy creaking of the spiritual joints of the body of Christ. Here, there doesn't appear to be any creaking in any joints, it's just amazing! A wonderful time in the history of Israel. Joshua was greatly privileged and was the right man for Israel at the time. Clearly, God chose him and put him into place.

SECTION X:
THE CITY, THE INHABITANT, THE SPIES

chapter thirty-eight
INTRODUCTION TO JERICHO

Jericho is Joshua, and Joshua is Jericho. We can't speak of one without mentioning the other. We will spend time with this passage around Jericho and the early times in Canaan. This will help us to understand why God is against them. Here we will find some things perfectly well understood and familiar to us today. *Sin is the human constant throughout the ages.*

The Book of Joshua chapter 2

It is in the second chapter of the book of Joshua that sees him grow in stature. The Jordan and Jericho ratify Joshua as Moses's successor. More importantly, they show that he is God's man for this time.

Israel was on the Plains of Moab before the Jordan. This is the moment God prepared since Abraham. It is the moment this nation had been anticipating for hundreds of years. Israel was here before! Not at the exact same place but close enough. Joshua is about to send two spies into Canaan. Moses had sent twelve. Ten of Moses's spies only saw giants and danger. Two of them saw a land full of milk and honey. Perhaps Joshua only commissioned two spies in order to send this message: "Come back with the same response as the two original spies, Joshua himself and Caleb." We know that *"In the multitude of counsellors there is safety"* (Prov 11:14). But perhaps two, full of faith, make a good committee!

Joshua didn't want to hear about what men couldn't do for themselves or even for God. Joshua wanted to know what God could do for men, by Himself. A stark contrast exists between the eyes of faith and the eyes of unbelief. One sucks the life of God out of us while the other injects spiritual life into us.

The two spies must go "*secretly.*" It is incumbent upon us to be discrete when discretion is mandated, as in the theatre of war. This is the beginning of the story of the mature Joshua. However, the story quickly leaves him and turns to a beautiful Bible character, the harlot Rahab.

chapter thirty-nine
BEING THE HOME OF RAHAB

The first city identified in Canaan is Jericho. Sadly, it was representative of every city in Canaan and many cities throughout time. The 'city' is the home of wickedness.

Believers look for a new city, the City of God, the New Jerusalem, a heavenly city not built with hands. The Apostle Peter states this plainly. *"Nevertheless we, according to His promise, look for new heavens and a new earth in which righteousness dwells"* (2 Peter 3:13).

The story turns too quickly to this sad city. We didn't want to go there! Who wants to read of the corruption of men and women at their grubbiest level? Who wants to delve into the subjection and abuse of women? We dearly wanted to discover Joshua and his exploits, but first we must consider Canaanite society. The church desperately needs to face up to the reality of sin. We need to understand why God commanded that the cities of Canaan be invaded and destroyed. We need to glorify God for his righteous judgments in the earth and learn righteousness.

It is a serious thing to realize that the evidence of moral and ethical decline in Jericho is like the cities of our present day. Remember that morals and ethics follow from faith and belief. The greater the void of these things, the greater the sin. So, let's pull ourselves together and take a cold, hard look at Jericho through the eyes of one—Rahab the harlot. Before you question God's judgements, meditate on the evil of the cities.

The spies lodged in her house on the city wall. She lived at her place of business. The term here translated as 'harlot's house' can also be translated 'tavern' or 'hostess.' However, try as we might to ease back on Rahab's reputation, it is difficult. History has universally accepted the obvious reading of the text. Some, recently, tried to argue for a respectable title for Rahab by preferring 'hostess' or 'tavern owner.' However, any reader can see that all three renderings give reasonable cause to accept her title as Rahab the harlot. All three references suggest the same idea: like a hostess in the old Wild West! Or in Rome or Great Britain. Rahab the 'harlot' is the honest introduction to the city of Jericho.

As Joshua and Jericho are inseparable so Joshua and Rahab are inseparable. We can't mention one without thinking of the other. She is the only person remembered from the once great city. She stands with Joshua for all time. He happily stands with her. Her achievement and character shine through the ages and are so powerful that even her title became sanctified when describing her. Rahab the harlot will be in heaven. There, she will have a new name, better than the old one. There are no harlots in the City of God, the New Jerusalem. The Bible says, *"... you shall be called by a new name which the mouth of the Lord will name"* (Isaiah 62:2), *"...and a new name..."* (Revelation 2:17). Rahab would doubtless be glad of a new name. The old life with its sins is already forgiven. Rahab's faith produced works: evidence of God-given faith. Rahab would also be glad to be free of the very memory of her past. She will carry it, so to speak, like Ruth the Moabitess, for as long as it brings glory to God who redeemed her. Then her true beauty will be set free to shine a light on her life that will dispel all its past darkness.

chapter forty
BEING HIDDEN

Someone reported the two men who visited Rahab... hmm? Who would do that!? Probably it was a regular visitor to Rahab's house, someone familiar with Israelite characteristics, facial details, attitudes, mannerisms. Or, more likely, someone familiar with the surroundings and patterns of Rahab's establishment. They were regulars there, familiar enough to recognize a new customer. Most visitors would be ashamed of being recognized. People who are hiding can't see what is going on around them. But not this 'reporter.' Perhaps, therefore, it was the man who organized business for Rahab, who therefore knew everyone who sneaked in there. He perhaps could have access to the king if he had information of interest. Or perhaps the king himself was a regular visitor. The reporter may have also had leverage over the king. Bribery is an ancient 'profession.' The sins of the flesh are timeless.

And so, Rahab receives a visit from the king's servants. It's likely that nobody cared about 'normal' visitors to Rahab. It was just accepted with the other wicked acts of Jericho. Perhaps the spies hid their faces unlike the regulars whose conscience had long since been "*...seared with a hot iron*" (1 Timothy 4:2). Had the spies not been different in behaviour, they wouldn't have been singled out. The fact that they identified them as spies from Israel tells us something more.

Israel hadn't crossed the Jordan yet. But word of their intentions had reached Jericho. Jericho was on a nervous, unspoken alert. We might reasonably assume their consciences were thoroughly dead (1 Timothy 4:2). But they were alive to fear, pain, and death.

Soft living reduces discipline and leads to sin. Sinning produces an inability to fight anything.

Verse 3

See this laziness in the men the king sent to Rahab's house. They didn't storm in intending to drag the spies out. They told Rahab to bring them out. They didn't even go into Rahab's house even though they were there at the king's command! Rahab herself was to drag them out?! What is going on here? The men surely weren't afraid of the spies. Is it possible they were afraid of Rahab?! They likely feared Rahab more than Israel at this moment. Rahab had learned the power of sensitive information. The underworld has always known the power of exposure, blackmail, and ruin. Nobody said anything about Rahab's house. That was the rule—a society of mutual mutes. A community hung around Rahab's house where the only thing you couldn't do was speak. If you did, you might open a sewer that could produce endless reverberations throughout the city. Thus… making the man who reported the spies interesting to us.

This man must have had a special familiarity with Rahab's clientele. He also wasn't afraid to go to the king. This 'someone,' we may reasonably ask, could have been the man who arranged the king's visits to Rahab. Why didn't the king send his guard to storm the place? Because he too was afraid of Rahab and what she could do to him. Rahab's clientele slept peaceably only because of her discretion. Some things never change! This little cameo of Jericho sums up the whole character of the city. A city full of lies and deceit. A city full of hypocrisy and cheating. A city with an underworld, a vulnerable underbelly. A city whose foundations were rotted away by abuse and vice. The men from the king nervously demanded that Rahab bring out the two spies.

chapter forty-one
RAHAB AND THE KING

Verses 4 and 5

Now Rahab had somehow established that these men were different. Without doubt, Rahab could read men! She would have seen something different. Their poise, a different sense of purpose, a different look in their eyes. How often do our eyes expose us? Something told her these were not her normal clients. She knew what men looked like when they were ashamed. These men were hiding but they weren't ashamed! Perhaps Rahab sensed this, and it would seem she had similar thoughts as the man who went to the king. She didn't have to wait long. Ironically, the king's men confirmed all she had thought. They filled in the gaps; these men were spies, and Rahab was told to deliver them. What bravery is shown by Rahab in this society. But note how God allows men to suffer for their evil, to reap that which they have sown. They will reap a whirlwind of God's judgement.

Rahab's response is very clever. It's also thoroughly dishonest! What possible justification can God have for using her? Well... it seems to me that the men of Jericho had made her the channel for God's judgement. Rahab did what these men always wanted her to do. She told lies. They never wanted truth, not even the king. Especially not the king! These men made Rahab a specialist at deception... and deceiving themselves. They gave her the title The Harlot Rahab. God used it to fulfil His purpose and to redeem her. Only God could have inspired such a set of circumstances. God turned the title they had given her into the tool used for their destruction. When we read *"Rahab the Harlot"* today, we don't hear condemnation. We hear praise for a righteous God who delivers sinners from their oppressors and turns them into saints.

She says two men came but left, but she doesn't know where they went, saying they went out after dark... lies! She then tells them to go and catch them. With a blindness that had become their nature, they go. However, Rahab had hidden them—God had hidden them—on the roof among stalks of flax. Why does the Bible tell us about stalks of flacks in the middle of this tense episode?

chapter forty-two

A VIRTUOUS WOMAN

Flax was a plant from which linen was made. The fibres from the stem of the plant are the most ancient of textile fibres. Flax provided the linen threads for the swaddling clothes of the infant Jesus and His burial wrappings. These men were wrapped among these stalks of flax and kept safe, just as Christ would be. The Son of God would leave behind a set of linen garments folded neatly when He rose in power at the resurrection. Surely Rahab might be seen in Isaiah as that "...*smoking flax He will not quench*" (Isaiah 42:3). Her life was always in the balance and under threat from wicked men. It was even now under threat from the armies of God. But God wouldn't allow her humble life to be "*quenched.*" He would take it and use it for His glory. It would remain in the annuls of God's Holy Word for all time. King Solomon, the wisest man who ever, lived describes a "Virtuous woman." "*Her worth is far above rubies... her husband safely trusts her... She does him good and not evil all the days of her life. She seeks wool and flax and willingly works with her hands...*" (Prov. 31:10-13). See that woman, and then see Rahab. Rahab has all the characteristics Solomon speaks of. But she was reduced to a harlot by Jericho. Observe the purity and worth in Solomon's description... then see that same woman in her prime, robbed of everything she was meant to be by wicked men. I wonder if the Lord had Rahab in mind when he inspired King Solomon to write these words... a virtuous woman finds flax and labours cheerfully.

Proverbs says her husband will have no need to use unlawful means to earn his livelihood. Then see the goodness of God in his dealings with this sole survivor of the wicked city of Jericho as quoted from Zondervan's pictorial Bible Dictionary:

Jewish tradition held Rahab in high honour. One tradition making her the wife of Joshua. According to Matthews genealogy Rahab is one of the four women mentioned in the line of Christ. She is also the mother of Boaz, (a very wealthy man) the husband of Ruth, the grandmother therefore of King David (Matt 1:5; Ruth 4: 18-20). James shows his appreciation of her as a person in whom faith was not merely theological but practical as well (James 2:25).[4]

---

4 Merill Tenney, *Zondervan's Pictorial Bible Dictionary* (Grand Rapids, Michigan: Zondervan, 1967), 703.

chapter forty-three

BEING BREACHED

Verse 7

As soon as the searchers left they shut the gate to provide themselves a sense of security, desperate because they had been violated! Someone had spied upon them. They had seen all manner of evil spilling out into the streets and the countryside. In every hamlet sin saturated Jericho. The whole land of Canaan was typified here in the details of Jericho. They imagined themselves liberated and free, but their bondage was visible as far away as heaven.

They were comfortable in silently licensing each other to sin, congratulating themselves for their mutual blindness. But they had been breached! Can you feel their tension as they shut the city gate? The Bible tells us *"...as soon as those who pursued them had gone out, they shut the gate"* (Joshua 2:7). Like the cold wind on a winter's night makes you shudder, so these men shuddered at the thought of spies in their city. Who were the two men? Fear is honed to read circumstances well. Their long, dead consciences jerked a momentary confirmation. Wicked people are afraid of their own shadows... but these spies were real...

chapter forty-four

TIME TO REPENT

Here we are given the picture of what it was like to live in Jericho. Since Israel left Egypt forty years earlier, Jericho had been warned to repent. Jericho should have been invaded under Moses's reign, but God's people refused to go. Oh, what judgement lay upon that generation for failing to obey God. Rahab might have been saved forty years of misery! How many of us have been afraid of telling someone the hope of the gospel and left the sinner in their hopelessness. "... *having no hope and without God in the world*" (Ephes. 2:12).

God gives us time to change. Jericho had been told about the miracles, the deliverances, and the acts of God on behalf of Israel. All of these had been sent round the ancient world's oral communications systems. (Technology is overrated!) Everybody in Canaan knew who Israel was and what kind of God Jehovah was. But they didn't change. They continued and persisted in evil. Now, after forty years, the God of Israel was on the other side of Jordan again—too close to allow for an evil conscience to quell righteous terror. We can't imagine the evil that would have befallen the spies and Rahab had they been found. Rahab knew; she had been subject to their evil tempers for a long time.

Rahab recounts for the spies what the understanding is in Jericho. "*The inhabitants of the land are fainthearted because of you*" (Joshua 2:9). The talk in Canaan for over forty years had been about Israel and a righteous God and His judgements. It was about how invincible Israel was when they followed their God.

chapter forty-five

BEING TALKED ABOUT

When people see God's children walking with Him, they talk about it! Why aren't people talking about the church today? Well we may ask! But know this... something is wrong when the world isn't talking about the church. The New Testament world observed God's church in action: "... *these who have turned the world upside down...*" (Acts 17:6). Jericho was about to be turned inside out!

Today the church doesn't want to be seen by the world as 'terrifying.' We want to be seen 'nurse like,' gliding to tend the sinners' wounds and make them comfortable. God sees the world as needy and oppressed by sin, in need of deliverance, but also as rebellious. Men blame God for every evil that they cause, trying desperately to replace Him with themselves! Yet all the while He listens. He hears every blasphemy, and yet "*...God demonstrates His own love toward us, in that while we were still sinners, Christ died for us*" (Romans 5:8).

Calculate for yourself how many cutting blasphemies cross your path, and you ignore the stab they are to the Christ within you. God wants to send an army with banners to assault evil with righteousness, to call people to repentance and peace with God. God wants strong men like Joshua to 'stand up for Jesus,' knowing that there go I but for the grace of God. How many oppressed people would lift their eyes to heaven and give thanks were the church to declare God's judgements, God's justice, and God's salvation? The gospel is a full message. Rahab did not think God was unjust.

When we read about Joshua in these early verses, he is a distinct being. He is a man, yes, but strong, capable, and proven. He is focussed on doing the will of God no matter the cost. He is a fearless man. Joshua knows that God is with him. He knows his task is righteous. He knows his enemies are unrighteous in all they do. He is a believer! He is a servant of God. As Jericho comes nearer Joshua becomes stronger. As Joshua comes closer, Jericho becomes weaker. "*Our hearts melted*" (Joshua 2:11), says Rahab.

chapter forty-six

RAHAB'S PROFESSION OF FAITH

The reasons people turn to the Lord can sometimes be suspect. Many people make a profession of faith to get the benefits of the church's generosity. Rahab didn't want to die. She might be under suspicion in this regard. Is there evidence of a deeper work in her heart? I think there is. She says, "... *I know that the Lord has given you the land...*" (Joshua 2:9). This statement is clearly the result of some hard thinking. Note her use of God in verse 10 as, "... *the Lord... dried up the water of the Red Sea...*" Also, verse 11 might easily be taken as a statement of faith: "... *the Lord your God He is God, He is God in heaven above and on earth beneath.*" These are all good expressions, but evidence to support words is necessary.

One evidence of a real work of God in the heart of a sinner is that they stop being self-centred. They do what Jesus says "... *love the Lord your God... [and] your neighbour as yourself*" (Matt 22:36-40). Rahab appeals for her family's safety, not just her own. She says, "... *also... my father's house...*" (Joshua 2:12). Rahab expands on "family" in verse 13, "... *my father, my mother, my brothers, my sisters, and all that they have...*" Rahab is spreading the love of God, beginning at home. She becomes more attractive to the reader as the story proceeds. Perhaps Rahab's family disowned her because of her manner of life. Perhaps they lost touch deliberately. Here, the black sheep of the family becomes their salvation. That is... if they will listen and obey her challenging call to come to her house of ill repute!

Be careful not to let a desperation for results stop your critical thinking when it comes to professions of faith. We don't despise the day of small things, but we must have standards that set the norms. Note that God expects Rahab's family to go to her house if they would be saved. Often God's Church has been seen as a despised place. Yet God has never left it, and it is the closest place to heaven on earth. Don't be ashamed of it. Don't try to make it something it was never meant to be.

chapter forty-seven

A SIMPLE RED CORD

Verses 12–16

The spies made a deal with Rahab—her life for theirs, and they would save her when they returned. She couldn't tell anyone about them. Now I have probably made too much of this point already, but if anyone in Jericho knew how to keep a secret, Rahab was that person! Here, God turned Rahab's wicked 'degree in lies' into the keepsake of His purposes. Rahab can't be condemned—she had only just met God's servants and recently became a follower of God. We can't expect a lifetime of sin to be expunged in a few weeks. Sanctification is a lifelong process, even in the life of believers from good Christian homes. Rahab had none of these advantages. She reverted momentarily to the type of person Jericho had made her. To confuse the enemies of Israel, the Lord simply removed his hand from restraining Rahab, letting them experience what they had produced... lies and deceit... and destruction.

Rahab told the spies to go to the mountains for three days by which time the pursuers would have returned. Likewise, Rahab asked for a clear token that they would save her and her family. She wanted an assurance, a guarantee, a solid hope. What use is salvation without assurance? She lets them down and they have a final word as they go. Assurance is essential for believers of every sort but particularly leaders. It shapes the person. Without assurance we can't speak with confidence. Confidence without assurance is mere blustering!

Being Joshua

Verses 17–21

They give her a simple red cord to be hung out of her window. Only those who stayed in her house would be saved. The spies would take full responsibility for anyone inside. They disowned responsibility for anyone outside of the house... backslider be warned! They left, and she tied the red cord to the window. Can you imagine how she felt? God wouldn't fail Rahab. He will not fail you.

The worry in the city and its inhabitants abated, and the spies were not found. All that is left to expose the threat to Jericho and to declare Rahab's hope is a red thread hanging on the outside of the great city's wall. It declared that God would save His people even in Jericho. Jericho ignored the red cord! The colour red has signified 'blood' in every culture and society throughout time. Blood red is a universal statement. Israel would instantly recall the blood on the lintels and door posts of their homes in Egypt on the night the Angel of Death passed over them. That is the point... the angel 'passed' over them! Exodus 12:7 says, *"take some of the blood... on the two doorposts and on the lintel of your houses."* Then, in Exodus 12:13, God says, *"... when I see the blood, I will pass over you; and the plague shall not be on you to destroy you when I strike the land of Egypt."* Red blood stayed the hand of God. The blood of the Passover lamb was symbolic of Christ's redeeming blood.

Rahab's red cord will stay the hand of the Israelite soldiers executing God's judgement upon Jericho. These men were aware of the significance of this amazing colour. Many of them were the firstborn of their families in Egypt who would have died that Passover night, but for the red blood! All believers reading this story are struck by the significance of the red cord. Rahab's house would not experience death. No blood would be shed in Rahab's house.

There can be no doubt that this is a little cameo of the church of Jesus Christ trusting in His shed blood as judgement nears this world. Together they cling to this firm hope that God's avenging angel will see the blood. Here the Israelite soldiers would see Rahab's red cord hanging from the window and not dispense judgement there.

A Simple Red Cord

The story points all of us to the blood of Christ shed on the Cross of Calvary, which must be applied by faith to our hearts for God's judgement to pass over us. Do you, dear reader, have such a hope of salvation? You can find it only in Jesus Christ.

Can we imagine Rahab treating this red cord carelessly? No—this was now the most precious item she had! That scarlet cord runs through the history of salvation from Genesis to Revelation. It is the story of our redemption.

Here, the heart of Joshua was also revealed. The spies were protecting those who weren't Joshua's enemies—there were lots of windows on the wall—but only one would have a red cord. In this story, the gospel is illustrated at the beginning of God's judgement falling on Jericho. Before judgement, God set His own apart for salvation. As the army of Israel marched around Jericho, they would note that red cord on the wall. It would be foremost in their minds as the battle rages. As judgement fell upon Jericho, Rahab might have been afraid, even doubtful, but she wouldn't be lost. Joshua kept His promise. So does God.

SECTION XI:
THE CITY

chapter forty-eight

THE RISE OF CITIES

The Book of Genesis tells of the growth of mankind. From one man to a man and a woman, then came the family, children, and the extended family... into generations and population explosion. Growth also went from a garden to a home to a community, from a village to a town and on... the creation of the city and the state, the nations. The city might be the fulcrum of human society with the family and the nations at opposing extremities. The biblical story tells of the rise of great cities and of their fall, from Babel, to Sodom and Gomorrah, to Jericho right on to Jerusalem the city of God with Israel's greatest king, King David.

We can see the city's role in the New Testament as Jesus walked city streets preaching the gospel of the kingdom. Countless great cities have risen and fallen in history. We can admire the feats of men. Human genius designed and built the cities. The same human genius built the tools of war that destroyed them. The "city," as an ideal, has its ultimate fulfillment in the book of "The Revelation of Saint John the Divine." This city is incomparable and eternal. It is the only 'eternal city.' I include a lengthy quote to compare it with the cities of men.

> the great city, the holy Jerusalem, descending out of heaven from God, having the glory of God. Her light was like a most precious stone, like a jasper stone, clear as crystal. Also she had a great and high wall with twelve gates, and twelve angels at the gates, and names written on them, which are the names of the twelve tribes of the children

of Israel: three gates on the east, three gates on the north, three gates on the south, and three gates on the west.

Now the wall of the city had twelve foundations, and on them were the names of the twelve apostles of the Lamb. And he who talked with me had a gold reed to measure the city, its gates, and its wall. The city is laid out as a square; its length is as great as its breadth. And he measured the city with the reed: twelve thousand furlongs. Its length, breadth, and height are equal. Then he measured its wall: one hundred and forty-four cubits, according to the measure of a man, that is, of an angel. The construction of its wall was of jasper; and the city was pure gold, like clear glass. The foundations of the wall of the city were adorned with all kinds of precious stones: the first foundation was jasper, the second sapphire, the third chalcedony, the fourth emerald, the fifth sardonyx, the sixth sardius, the seventh chrysolite, the eighth beryl, the ninth topaz, the tenth chrysoprase, the eleventh jacinth, and the twelfth amethyst. The twelve gates were twelve pearls: each individual gate was of one pearl. And the street of the city was pure gold, like transparent glass. But I saw no temple in it, for the Lord God Almighty and the Lamb are its temple. The city had no need of the sun or of the moon to shine in it, for the glory of God illuminated it. The Lamb is its light.

—Revelation 21:10–23

chapter forty-nine

THE CITY (PART 1)

In "*The City of God,*" Augustine (Ad 354–430) takes the idea of two cities to illustrate two basic human conditions, two types of mankind. The term he uses includes men and women. These two cities function simultaneously in the world. Two opposing forces drive them. One is the city of this world; the other is the city of God. He shows these two principles in different ways. He observes that the Bible tells us Cain, being worldly, founded a city. His brother Abel did not because he was a pilgrim, a stranger in this world. Cain was of the city of man and Abel was of the city of God. The city of the world is here and is wicked. Pilgrims like Abel also have a city but in the heavens where Christ is. *"For we know that if our earthly house, this tent, is destroyed, we have a building from God, a house not made with hands, eternal in the heavens"* (2 Corinthians 5:1). In this world, the pilgrims are foreigners in a foreign land. They are believers and God's people. Some of them are still in the city of the world, but God will redeem them in His good time.

Genesis 6 begins with the words: "… *when men began to multiply on the face of the earth…*" (Genesis 6:1). These words carry an ominous tone. Perhaps due to our prior reading of the story, but maybe not. It might be an innate sense, an inbred fear, warning us that trouble is brewing every time men begin to multiply. T. Chalmers talks about "…the guilty history of every place of crowded population."[5]

---

5 T. Chalmers, *Preahcers Homiletic Commentary, Vol 28, Ephesians* (Grand Rapids, Michigan: Baker Book House, 1974), 251.

One aspect of the problem of cities is the strangely powerful effect of numbers on the individual. We have discussed the weaknesses of our modern cultural individualism. Cities are the opposite, but equally problematic. There are significantly smaller populations in the country. Take a trip into most villages, and you will be confronted by a stillness that actually helps you to think. Many people go to the countryside for rest and refreshment. This is available in most country places for the very reason that it isn't available in the cities. There are no crowds in small villages. If there are, it is for a happy event like a fair, or an annual event where everybody comes out in support of each other's project. In the city, the individual can't get space to think. Everywhere in the city unsubstantiated opinions are intruding upon you.

Eventually the individual stops trying to think for the noise and aggression and slumbers into a bed of conformity, laying aside personal thoughts, becoming a clone, unable to think freely for himself. Those who manage to retain free thought and speech are seen as strange or disruptive to the norm. Today they are seen as dangerous. They threaten the boring norm of one population thinking only one thought.

Cities take on a uniform character. Strangely, this inability to think for yourself produces a wide-open door to receive the thoughts of others, including every evil under the sun. This is one reason why cities gather and protect all sorts of weirdness and extremes... The cramped closeness of the inhabitants inherently produces problems. There are boundaries in cities, but they are paper thin!

Much noise in the city seems to achieve the silencing of consciences, and so doing, exacerbates the moral decline of all who live there. No one can speak. Discussion? There's no time for serious examination of essentials. Everything feeds everything else... to death! Cities are a whirlwind that lifts people up into a fantasy sky, then drops them from a great height to their destruction.

chapter fifty
THE CITY (PART 2)

Chalmers counsels parents to make sure they have admonished their children about the deceit, distortion and evil that exists in cities. He says soberly that parents are bound to fortify their children with the intellectual and spiritual means to compete with these evils. We must give our children answers, and train and strengthen them against the albeit flimsy claims of the city. Every parent knows this guilty history of the city. [6]

The countryside offers a much more wholesome reality. A connection to nature which 'declares the glory of God.' Cities declare the glory of men, even as both the city and its builders degenerate. The countryside inspires thought and freedom and slows everything down to the rate of the seasons.

Familiarity of families and helpful caring is obviously required when there are fewer people, and enriching individualism can flourish in the country. Cities are faceless. They demand a lifeless conformity, a corporate identity, typified in the non-personal form to fill in for everything... online. In the countryside, you walk down the street to the doctor who played soccer with your dad and who brought you into the world fifty years ago!

Would to God that the countryside was perfect. Sadly, the fall affected us all. Another story could be told of the countryside, but the relevant aspect for Joshua and the destruction of Jericho is the one here mentioned. The countryside around Jericho wouldn't miss the spilling out of the city onto its gentle fields and pastures and

---

6 T. Chalmers, *Preachers*, 251.

rivers. They would breathe cleaner air and drink purer water from now on. But morally the only difference between the city and the countryside is opportunity. Both are guilty of maximizing it.

Here are a few verses that sum up the human condition. "*... for all have sinned and fall short of the glory of God*" (Romans 3:23). "*There is none righteous, no, not one; There is none who understands; There is none who seeks after God*" (Romans 3:10–11). Isaiah personalizes the matter "*... we are all like an unclean thing and all our righteousnesses are like filthy rags; we all fade as a leaf, and our iniquities, like the wind, have taken us away*" (Isaiah 64:6).

Parents fear for their children when they leave home to study or live in the city. Parents themselves were probably infected by urban venom when they were teenagers. Cities don't give rise to noble living. As noted, they are seething caldrons of filth. Yet today young Christian men and women are often comfortable there. Of course, there is another side to cities. There are many decent folk in cities. But they must turn a blind eye to what is happening after dark on their doorstep. Many city dwellers today, just like Job, are "*...oppressed by the filthy conduct of the wicked*" (2 Peter 2:8).

chapter fifty-one

A GENERATION OF DEGRADATION

Tell me this... did the city's morals improve from forty years earlier when Joshua came as a spy? No, it was worse. When Israel turned to wandering in the desert forty years earlier, Jericho was energized to enjoy its sins even more. The result was that sin spoiled its men of war. Even giants get fat. They lost their fight by giving in to sin daily. They mislaid their weapons, and they were too heavy to lift when they found them.

Jericho was wicked before Joshua went to Canaan as one of the twelve spies. We can see this from the report of the ten spies who were afraid to go up due to the ferocity of the inhabitants. Jericho was vicious to its people. In the intervening years, God bestowed awesome harvests and great blessings. He sends blessings to bring us to repentance. But they refused. Now he would send Israel to punish them. The blessings of the land would be given to those who were more worthy than the Canaanites. Jericho had been decadent for decades.

Numbers 13:32 says, *"... the land through which we have gone to spy is a land that devours its inhabitants."* This phrase sums up the dreadful state in Jericho. How often nations collapse due to sin amid fullness. History is replete with examples of what we are being told here about Jericho. Interestingly, Jericho is regarded as at least one of the first great cities, if not the first great city. When God punishes the wicked, it is only after long-suffering and many warnings. Only when His advances have been spurned does God send irreversible judgment.

They feared nothing, and no challenge existed to their way of life until this nation of slaves escaped Egypt. Israel's Exodus was talked about with trepidation among the wicked. Israel had grown strong in their desert wanderings under Moses and developed into a nation of note. See the description Rahab gives of this *"devouring"* city now that forty years have passed:

> *the terror of you has fallen on us, and that all the inhabitants of the land are fainthearted because of you.*
> —Joshua 2:9

> *As soon as we heard these things, our hearts melted; neither did there remain any more courage in anyone because of you, for the Lord your God, He is God in heaven above and on earth beneath.*
> —Joshua 2:11

> *truly the Lord, has delivered all the land into our hands, for indeed all the inhabitants of the country are fainthearted because of us.*
> —Joshua 2:24

Evil eats away the vitals of the individual and the community from the highest level down.

The spies returned with a different message then the previous ten spies. They tell Joshua that Jericho has changed over these forty years. The repeated picture is that the inhabitants of the land are given to terror because of Israel.

Genesis 6:5 says, *"Then the Lord saw that the wickedness of man was great in the earth, and that every intent of the thoughts of his heart was only evil continually."* These ancient warnings about sin and judgement ought to caution men. But men today, like then, don't learn from history, as a matter of course, but from moral history… as a matter of choice!

chapter fifty-two

GOD BEING ANGRY

So, the Bible gives its justification for the removal of a moral epidemic. Jericho's only named inhabitant testifies of its evils and its lack of response to God's blessings. God will now take these blessings and give them to others more worthy. Joshua will oversee this cleansing of the land of Canaan. He understands how God works.

However, as a believer and a Bible reader, we know God is good. We know He is long-suffering. We understand that if God judges a city, it's for good reason. The believer doesn't doubt the justice of God or His actions towards men. We believe and therefore we understand. But we have also seen His undeserved mercy poured out on our own lives.

Augustine comments on God's judgement remind us that divine anger isn't like human anger. Human anger is generally an emotional outburst. A characteristic of this outburst is a sense of remorse following it. Augustine says: "The anger of God is no violent emotion, but the due judgement of sin that demands punishment. God does not regret what He has done. Just as he has a firm knowledge of everything before it happens, so His opinion of it when it happens, remains unchanged." Augustine goes on to point out what the Bible means when it describes God as "Angry". The Bible uses anthropomorphic language (communication reduced to the human level) God never changes. The language that threatens us of God's judgements is used to "Terrify the proud and arouse the careless, answer the inquirers and satisfy the intelligent. This it (the scriptures) could not do unless it first stooped and condescended to our low level".[7] Therefore, Augustine counsels us to: "…flee from the city of this world."[8]

---

7 Augustine, *City of God book XV*, 261.
8 Augustine, *City of God book XVIII*, 290.

SECTION XII: THE JORDAN CROSSING

chapter fifty-three
PREPARATION FOR PUNISHMENT

Joshua 3:1ff

And so, God arose to judge Jericho. Joshua also rises early, like every man who ever was serious about life and God. They move and camp before the Jordan river. The text says thoughtfully that they "... *lodged there before they crossed over*" (Joshua 3:1). In this "lodging," there is no sense of reconsidering. We are observing a deliberate pause to weigh the event. It's the final breath before taking the plunge into something big. This pause for the believer, is before God. Carelessness in the believer's life is brought to heel by moments of waiting upon God.

Joshua 3:2 says this waiting lasted three days. Time enough for the people of God to prepare for battle. The people of Jericho wouldn't prepare for battle. Jericho would simply 'melt' as their fear intensified. Nineveh, another great and wicked city, repented in sackcloth and ashes when faced with destruction and would be spared by God's mercy (Jonah chapter 4). But Jericho had no thought of repentance. *Evil energizes men when they most need restraint. It paralyzes them when they most need action.* Jericho should have restrained its evil practices but did not. Right now, they should be at least energizing themselves to defend their city, but they are not. God's judgements are the result of man's actions. When God's judgements are in the world men learn righteousness. The innocent in society benefit from God's judgements.

chapter fifty-four
KEEP YOUR DISTANCE

Joshua 3:3 takes our attention back to Israel and Joshua's campaign to take them into the Promised Land. They must watch the Ark of God. They followed it precisely in obedience, but also, so that they would know the route to take. Only God knows the way that we must take!

The Bible says to 'keep a distance' from the Ark. The command is strong: *"Do not come near it..."* (Joshua 3:4). This distance is essential to ensure that we don't end up in front of God, ahead of God's leading in our life. Joshua understood this. He likely learned it in the wilderness following the cloud by day and the fire by night. While today pastors are seen as leaders, God is looking for followers!

Jesus says "My *sheep hear my voice... and they follow me*" (John 10:27). It is the natural inclination of His sheep to follow Him.

Now Israel couldn't assume they knew enough to decide where to cross the river. God determined a particular spot to reveal Himself as the God of Israel. He has also determined to magnify Joshua before the nations. At this crossing, Joshua would be revealed as Moses's successor. Moses saw the nation miraculously over the Red Sea. Here Joshua would oversee a similar miracle, and the nation would know for certain that God is still with them.

Look for the Lord to confirm his support for your ministry before you enter a pulpit. Never look for God's hand just being evident to you. Others must recognize it. Be brave enough to ask them before you have made up your own mind. This idea of our direction and progress being determined by the Ark is hard to grasp. We are always in a hurry. We are always working to our own plan. We can do things. The church is frequently more spiritual when it is poor. Churches with money get into trouble.

chapter fifty-five

YOU HAVE NOT PASSED THIS WAY BEFORE

Concluding verse 4 we have this pert little sentence, easily passed over. It is a comment on our Christian walk, "...*for you have not passed this way before*" (Joshua 3:4). It isn't talking about taking a city or fighting a battle or being careful. It is simply the fact that they have never been where they are about to go, in spiritual terms!

Never assume that everything will be the same! God is always doing something fresh: "... *the Lord's mercies... are new every morning*" (Lam 3:22-23). Something about God's mercies is fresh and reviving. They are new, in that you have never seen them this way before. The church should never assume they understand everything about God or His ways.

Christian men in leadership must remind themselves that faith is set against sight. "... *we walk by faith not by sight*," says (2 Cor 5:7). We may recognize the terrain. But we don't know what God intends to accomplish. We can only follow the Ark, the leading of God's Holy Spirit.

This point is made at the outset of their entry to Canaan "*You have not passed this way before!*" It is sad to see old servants of God who have lost this edge. We can appear stale, repetitive, and at times plain boring. We often talk as though we know something about everything. We forget that God is not old. Beware when you find yourself using the phrase "in my experience"!

Do you want to see the freshness of God? Look at the seasons. For centuries, the seasonal changes bring gasps and awe as the colours change and temperatures fluctuate. Even in our familiar places, God is never boring. He has a purpose. He is working out a plan and everything is brought into His service to accomplish it. His mercies are new every morning (Lam 3:22,23).

chapter fifty-six

THIS JORDAN

Here *"this Jordan"* will provide a divine service as it breaks natures rules. It stopped flowing before the Ark of God. Nature rejoiced and happily bowed to His commands. Abraham, in heaven, rejoiced that morning. Hadn't God promised Him a seed and a land called Canaan? Here Abraham's seed stands ready to cross this Jordan. Moses, also in heaven, rejoiced to see Joshua lead God's people to their inheritance. Jericho was watching! Jericho wasn't rejoicing. Israel's arrival at the Jordan was a dark day. But their fear didn't turn them to repentance. It melted them like wax in intense heat.

We see the fulfillment of their faith and ours in Christ. On the cross, in the resurrection, and seated at the right hand of God interceding for us. Together we stand! Old and New Testament saints are one in Christ. We are the church of God, the body of Christ, one people. Each owns the other, and together we will rejoice around the throne of God, all redeemed by the precious blood of Christ. But not yet for them in their day, nor for us today. Just remember *"…you have not passed this way before."*

Pastor, leader, when you feel lonely or things are hard… remember that you are one with the saints in time. There really are saints in heaven, in some way we don't understand, following us in our trials and victories. In Hebrews 12:1, the writer talks of a great cloud of witnesses. This is not the saints themselves standing about watching us in all we do, like a divine TV show. It is the written Old Testament record he has just quoted at length in chapter 11. This record is a witness to us that they served well, and therefore, so should we. But the writer goes on to point us away from them to Christ

Himself. He is our source of energy as He was theirs. The idea of being part of a movement of great men and women, all of whom gained their energy from Christ Himself, is awesome. Their prayers we don't need, for Christ is interceding for us at the throne of God, but they encourage us by way of remembrance. They are good at encouragement; they all learned how to lift the spirits of their brethren when they were on this earth. All we need is the accounts of their exploits in the scriptures. We neither require nor benefit from images or icons, and they are doubtless offended when we venerate them. Christ is all and in all. The Jordan is Joshua's day he must rise and cross over. This is our day; we must likewise rise up and cross over whatever is before us.

chapter fifty-seven
SANCTIFICATION

"*Sanctify yourselves for tomorrow the Lord will do wonders among you*" (Joshua 3:5). Imagine the atmosphere in the camp of Israel?! Expect such experiences of God moving on your behalf.

Israel knew how to cross a river! What would we have accomplished at the Jordan? A boring bridge? A monument to our engineering skill? A statement about ourselves? There was no need for a bridge, God was among them. And their memory of the day lasted longer than the stones brought up from the Jordan. God intended to show His power. Pray that your church might covet such experiences with the living God. One reason for this lack of spiritual appetite is perhaps the principle expressed here. In order to see God's great works, we must sanctify ourselves.

The church needs Joshua's today—urgently. The world needs to see the people of God sanctify themselves and to see God again among His people. For a century, the Christian church has backed off and capitulated to the world. Desperate to find acceptance and desperate for recognition, for status among worldly men. Joshua would have been bewildered by us! He would have fully understood the Christian warfare to be spiritual. He would have understood the two-city motif. He would have understood that vast difference between the heathen and the people of God. He would have understood a loving God. He would have been bewildered with men who say they believe in Him without evidence. Joshua and the Nation of Israel are an example to us today. They issue a call to us to be one with them… to sanctify ourselves.

Sanctification. The word means set apart for holy use. The word indicates that which could do a lot of things, but it is only used for one special thing. If there is a shortage of tools, this tool remains locked away. It can't be used. There is a rigidity about sanctified things. Sanctification, in this respect, is restrictive. It is uncomfortable to be around. It reminds us of special things, moments, and people. A wife and a husband are, in a sense, sanctified people, set apart for one another—an institution instigated by God in the Garden of Eden.

Biblical sanctification is being set apart for God. This sanctification is called upon for the nation here at 'this Jordan.' Just a little river, but God was there. This wasn't a nation attempting to gain a new land. This enterprise was God fulfilling His promise to give them this land. It was just on the other side of Jordan. To enter it, they must sanctify themselves. When did you last do this? Deliberately, seriously, and determined to maintain it?

Consider before next Sunday morning worship at your church. Imagine, well imagination isn't a great way to start, but for now... imagine every church member today grasping this concept of sanctification. Israel knew what Joshua meant. Imagine if every church member obeyed this command of Joshua and got right with God! Repented, confessed, turned to Him, and gave themselves wholly to Him. Every day, every minute of every day right up to next Sunday! Imagine then, what would it be like at 'First Such and Such' a church?! We would expect something evident, something felt, to happen next Sunday morning. Surely, we might expect God to express His pleasure at our new dedication. To encourage us at least. What do you think would happen to you? Do you not think you might be quite a different person by the end of the week? You might be looking forward to worship in a special way? Well imagination is not, as I said, helpful. But one thing for certain—if Joshua called us to sanctify, he would expect a difference to be evident among us... tomorrow!! Tomorrow the Lord will do great thinks among you. Have expectations for your congregation.

A final note on this command to sanctify yourself. The Lord's working among us never comes as a result of anything in us. It is always a result of free grace. So, what is to be understood here is that the blessing will not come because of me, but it may not come because I am not ready for it. At this point in time, Joshua is ready, Israel is ready, Rahab is ready, God is ready... Jericho is absolutely not ready... this is how God works.

chapter fifty-eight

BEING EXALTED

"*Then Joshua spoke to the priests, saying, 'take up the ark of the covenant and cross over before the people...'*" (Joshua 3:6). Joshua now speaks to the priests. The priests obeyed: "*...So they took up the ark of the covenant and went before the people*" (3:6). God then speaks to Joshua, "*And the Lord said to Joshua, 'This day I will begin to exalt you in the sight of all Israel, that they may know that, as I was with Moses, so shall I be with you*" (3:7).

In this little cameo, we perhaps see a hierarchy of God's dealings with His people. The people are prepared, then the priests act. Joshua is ready, being a step ahead of both priests and people—surely a good pattern for a successful church. This is one nation of equals, all slaves, all delivered by the power of God, all equally necessary in their God-appointed places.

Why didn't the Lord just tell Joshua to do what Moses would have done? The Lord dealt with Joshua thus because Joshua and every successive generation must reinvent this 'wheel!' We must rediscover the power of God's Word for ourselves. Moses did, Joshua would too. The result will be similar in us, a confidence in God's Word, but the experience of the user will always be fresh. God make us and keep us fresh!

chapter fifty-nine

BEING ABLE TO STAND IN YOUR JORDAN

Joshua 3:8

"*You shall command the priests who bear the ark of the covenant saying, 'when you have come to the edge of the water of the Jordan, you shall stand in the Jordan.'*"

These two words are interesting, *"stand in"* the Jordan. So, what was this Jordan? For Joshua, it was his final test of faith as Moses's successor. (Not his last.) For the priests, this Jordan was a challenge of obedience. For God, it was nature showing its willingness to serve its creator. It was also a divine declaration about God's servant Joshua. God would show the world that as He was with Moses so would He be with Joshua. Jericho was watching. All of Canaan was listening.

There is never just one thing going on with God. The actual walking across the riverbed was spectacular. It might terrify the Canaanites. But it was perhaps the least important event! It's just a river God made a long time ago. Getting the Jordan to stop flowing is no problem at all. He got it flowing in the first place didn't he? However, bringing all the other aspects into place required years of dealings in the desert. God had to bring people, priests, and Joshua, to this place of energetic trust and obedience. Men are God's most difficult task. Creation was easy then and easy now. Men were difficult then and difficult now. In these forty years, Israel had changed, Joshua had changed, and Jericho had changed. God remains eternally unchanged.

Joshua commanded as he was commanded to. The priests obeyed. The people watched in anticipation. Some no doubt doubted, some watched in bewilderment as they went along with everyone else. Some were enlivened by faith as they waited for God to show His power. Others still watched just for God Himself. His presence was always better than the miracle performed. The priests stood up to their ankles in the Jordan... in the problem.

Churches and individual believers sometimes find themselves up to their ankles in a problem. Here it was a problem created by God. He told them to go there! Most of the time we create and stand in problems of our own making. But God is always in control. Every 'Jordan' will take us somewhere better than where we are now. He planned it or allowed it to get you to where He wants you to be. We may fight and resist and try to get back to where we were, to the place before we stood in our Jordan, but the best thing, the right thing, is to wait on the Lord. He will tell you when it is time to step across and into your promised land. Remember that walking through the problem, this Jordan, would take them into the land of promise! *"When the Day of Pentecost had fully come, they were all with one accord in one place"* (Acts 2:1). There... He commands blessing!

In this passage we see Joshua's whole world engaged at the same time—Israel, the priests, and Joshua. Canaan was also fully engaged with what God is doing. Indeed, heaven was watching 'this Jordan.' All because God intended to exalt His servant Joshua in the eyes of His people, but also His people in the eyes of the heathen. The natural world is always busy in springtime, but not too busy to miss God's command. The Jordan would be stopped at its time of overflowing! It would start again only when God's people were safely in Canaan. This is the Promised Land—happening here in the Book of Joshua. These principles still apply today and pastors need to understand them to guide God's people into their Promised Land—any place of blessing God brings us to, including the eternal land promised to those who believe. *"For we know that if our earthly house, this tent, is destroyed, we have a building from God, a house not made with hands, eternal in the heavens."* (2 Cor 5:1).

SECTION XIII: OBEDIENCE, THE CEREMONY OF A BELIEVING HEART

chapter sixty
COME HERE AND HEAR

Joshua 3:9

Joshua uses an interesting choice of words in verse 9. He says, *"Come here, and hear..."* (Joshua 3:9). The intention was to express a sense of belonging and anticipation causing them to listen carefully. Joshua reveals himself to us in this little phrase as a man who knows God and men. *"Come here, and hear."*

Joshua watched the children of Israel listen in all sorts of different ways through their journeys. Men acquire a certain self-deception in the simple act of listening. He saw that merely using our ears isn't sufficient to produce the right response. He saw that understanding didn't guarantee the desired outcome. He perhaps also saw that when Israel was close with Moses and close with the Lord, everything worked to everyone's advantage and to the glory of God. Listening is affected by proximity. Make sure you are close to Him, where He is when He speaks. Make sure your closeness is never just emotional, but also the closeness of real affection. *Distance inspires disobedience. Proximity inspires obedience.*

In Joshua 3:10 and 11, Joshua draws the people to himself and explains what is about to happen. He tells them that they are going to receive a divine assurance of God's presence: *"... you shall know that the living God is among you"* (Joshua 3:10). And as Joshua was speaking, he was among the people. They drew near; they came when he called. Surely, Joshua was creating a picture of God's presence on his own. *"... He will without fail drive out from before you the Canaanites..."* (Joshua 3:10). He said they will know these things *"by this..."* He was referring to this remarkable mark of the divine presence with Israel... the Ark of the Covenant. The Ark would cross over the Jordan before them. God goes before His people. This is a biblical principle. This principle carries through into the Christian life. It reminds us that we are never called to travel uncharted waters. Jesus has already been there! He has been going before us in the person of the Holy Spirit to mark our way. Always look for the Lord up ahead on the rough road you are on. He is preparing a resting place for you. Rough roads that lead to where God is are ok! The rebellious sinner also has a rough road through life, but his end is worse than his beginning. Ours is to be with God, to see Jesus, never to miss Him again.

The truth is that my route has been trodden by the Lord Himself, to clear my way. What was impossible for me, He did. This is evident in the message of salvation presented in many ways in the Bible, all in perfect agreement. The basic message is that we can't save ourselves. We can't reach God or find reconciliation and acceptance with God, but by the work of Jesus Christ being our paschal lamb, being the scapegoat, being the offering, being our sin-bearer. The way to God became open for us by the blood of Christ. The obstacle of our sin, which we couldn't atone for, was atoned for by God's only Son.

God has trod your way. Your paths are written in His footsteps. Your burden is being supported by His almighty hand. Joshua encouraged the nation of Israel. He told them that God would take them through this impossibility to show them how he looks after them all the time. He is there in every moment. Especially when, in our moments of abject failure, we think perhaps He 'should' have left us. In these moments, He warmly says to us, *"Come here, and hear...I will go before you."* Wonderful words of love. Are you listening? The people are.

chapter sixty-one
FORTY YEARS TO TAKE A FEW STEPS

Joshua 3:12

They were told to take twelve men, one from each tribe. While there is ceremony in this event, it was, again, surprisingly minimal. Yet it was a moment of fulfillment for this nation, a moment promised centuries before—a moment held on to by faith and taught to children's children for centuries. It was a record kept pure without embellishment. Good journalism. These twelve men must have understood the moment they were in. While there is little ceremony, there was a lot of obedience. *Obedience is the ceremony of a believing heart.* They have a simple task, and they did it without question. They crossed the river.

You may have some idea of what it was like. You have had to trust God, to set the example, to make the first step of faith. How wonderful to watch those who follow. Perhaps generations of believers have come to faith since you came to Christ as the first member of your family to do so. You might have been a teenager; you never imagined the extent of the good influence that was going to have in the lives of others.

chapter sixty-two
TAKE A STAND ON THE PROBLEM

Joshua 3:14 *"So it was that when the people set out from their camp..."*

The story is told in some detail. So, what can we learn? The text draws our attention to the subject of 'timing.' "So it was that *"when!"* We must consider *"when"* the people moved out.

We are often ignorant about events that are happening around us. Many can't get beneath the surface of life. They think that what they see or what they know is all there is to know. In this moment, even Joshua didn't know what was going to happen. God does things when we obey Him. Often God won't move until He sees some movement in us. A movement that is generated by faith. The text explains my point when we put verses 14 and 16 together: *"So it was that when the people set out from the camp.... That the waters which came down for upstream stood still, and rose in a heap very far away at Adam..."* (Joshua 3:14,16)! At this moment, two things were happening: the connection is obedience and timing. The people move, then God moves. They move in obedience; He responds in miraculous power. We might preach this point by saying that it took forty years to get the people to take these few simple steps into the water.

How long has God been waiting on you to move from where you are? Have you been baptized yet? Is God waiting on you to do something you have been fighting against, like them, for forty years? God is only waiting on a few faith-filled steps. The people didn't know about the waters upstream. His people obeyed Joshua. They moved out from the camp... Then... He stopped the waters at Adam.

chapter sixty-three

GOD NEAR AT HAND AND GOD AFAR OFF

Between verses 14 and 16 there are also other things happening. The people move, and the priests bearing the Ark go before them. This movement culminates at the feet of the priests bearing the Ark of the covenant going into the Jordan. They just dipped in the edge. The waters had overflowed their banks and extended the width of the river. As soon as they all moved from the camp, the flow at Adam was stopped. The priest moved to the centre of the riverbed, and it was firm and dry in a very short time. The city of Adam was about eighteen miles north of Jericho.

See that the problem right under our feet can be solved from very far away. We are frequently stuck at the problem. God is never stuck. Long before the word 'remote' existed in daily communication, God worked remotely all the time. God always does new things. He improvises in His interventions. Nature is at His behest. That's just one of the reasons why we call Him "God."

In Joshua 3:17 the priests stood firm! There they were in the middle of the riverbed on dry land, and the people were gently, but hurriedly passing to the other side. They didn't move until all the people passed over. This is surely evidence that 'As I was with Moses, so shall I be with you.' God's approval doesn't depend on gifting or skills. God's approval is His anointing on us. When God gives an anointing, we might not be aware that we are anointed. This anointing is evidence of God's approval. Aim to have God's approval, not man's applause.

See also in verse 17, "...all Israel crossed over... all the people had crossed completely over the Jordan" (Joshua 3:17). Here is the

God we worship. He leaves no one behind. There were all sorts of people, some struggling at the tail end. All of them realized the waters would come back again. How many were filled with fear? How many with little faith, just holding on? Some were too busy rushing along to think. There must have been one person who was last to cross... I imagine him being encouraged, maybe even being carried the last few steps! The people cheering for him and calling out "don't quit!" "Trust the Lord!" "Just keep going!" I imagine as he stepped out of the dry riverbed a whole nation erupting into praise. Relief and sheer joy—the first event in Canaan being the cheering home of the last one of God's people crossing the Jordan. One older brother, the very last one. None were left behind; I imagine it might be me!

God won't fail us; He will stand by His promise and never leave us. Our trust is well placed if we trust only in Him. We shall be "saved!" That's the word to hang on to. Believe on the Lord Jesus Christ and "... *you will be saved*" (Rom 10:9). Not perhaps or maybe. Every soul trusting in Jesus Christ for their salvation will be saved for eternity. How would you have responded to this story if it concluded with the waters returning before some of God's people were able to cross? How would you feel if you were one of them? Perish the thought! But none of God's children will perish.

A gospel that allows God to lose some He saved? This is an insult to Almighty God. A 'gospel' not worthy of the Christian church. Certainly not found in the Bible. Such intensity of experience is to be expected in the life of the pastor from time to time. We shouldn't manufacture it but be alert when God sends it.

chapter sixty-four

MEMORIAL STONES

Then Joshua called the twelve men whom he had appointed from the children of Israel, one man from every tribe; and Joshua said to them: "Cross over before the ark of the Lord your God into the midst of the Jordan, and each one of you take up a stone on his shoulder, according to the number of the tribes of the children of Israel, that this may be a sign among you when your children ask in time to come, saying, 'What do these stones mean to you?' Then you shall answer them that the waters of the Jordan were cut off before the ark of the covenant of the Lord; when it crossed over the Jordan, the waters of the Jordan were cut off. And these stones shall be for a memorial to the children of Israel forever."

—Joshua 4:4-7

Now they had crossed over the Jordan. Abraham's seed, the children of Israel entered the Promised Land… at last! What do you think they should do now? How about some rejoicing? A music concert? A feast? Praise or worship? None of these. You see, God's vision for His church is more substantial than ours. Israel may have been thinking about their present arrival in Canaan. God is thinking about the future. We can be stuck in our present, but God is working a plan culminating in the cross and resurrection, the birth of the church and the coming of Christ and heaven. God doesn't have a five-year plan. He has a long-term plan… an eternal plan. Our planning must also be long-term!

Joshua, like the humble servant he is, took things a day at a time, but he had a long-term vision. God's servants must share God's vision. We must see beyond the present whether it be good or bad. So, the Lord's focus at the crossing of Jordan was that they bring up twelve stones to set up a simple monument. This for... the education of their children throughout future generations. God didn't set up a special program to minister to children. He told parents to teach their own children! We have superseded God's institution for the education of children. We have relieved parents of this responsibility, and the church has taken it over. A kind of socialist agenda where the church becomes big brother and does all the work—it is nowhere in the Bible. Teaching children is the parent's duty. An outreach to children may appear caring, but perhaps we should be winning their parents!

For God and for Joshua this day wasn't a moment of fulfillment or the end of something. It was the beginning of something. It wasn't the future of this generation alone. The future belongs to all the people. So now what should the subject of their attention be? While we could have chosen many things to celebrate on that day, God thought the most important issue, the urgent matter, was teaching our own... *children*!

Joshua chapter four ends with these words: *"that you may fear the Lord your God forever."* Another great purpose is also given: *"That all the peoples of the earth may know the hand of the Lord, that it is mighty, that you may fear the Lord your God Forever"* (Joshua 4:24). And so, let's look briefly at these stones...

chapter sixty-five

STONES THAT SPEAK

Take for yourselves twelve men from the people, one man from every tribe, and command them, saying, 'Take for yourselves twelve stones from here, out of the midst of the Jordan, from the place where the priests' feet stood firm. You shall carry them over with you and leave them in the lodging place where you lodge tonight.'... that this may be a sign among you when your children ask in time to come, saying, 'What do these stones mean to you?' Then you shall answer them that the waters of the Jordan were cut off before the ark of the covenant of the Lord; when it crossed over the Jordan, the waters of the Jordan were cut off. And these stones shall be for a memorial to the children of Israel forever.

—Joshua 4:2-7

The stones were placed like a cairn. A simple, visible memorial. The memorial had one specific purpose—to raise a question. It wasn't to raise worship or be an altar. It had no inherent value. If the cairn happened to be destroyed, it would be no great loss. Raising the question was its only function. If it couldn't raise that question, it was just a pile of useless stones. If it raised the question, it had fulfilled its purpose.

The stones can't answer the question. Dad must answer. These stones can't justify churches producing great works of art or complex, binding traditions. This simple pile of stones is much more useful. It doesn't bewilder the onlooker. It isn't concerned with atmosphere or profundity. It will go over the head of children. Thereby, it does raise a question, just one question. Many church traditions have superseded their usefulness. They simply represent the unknown and that's a relatively useless religious obsession. The gospel is that God 'revealed' Himself in the person of His Son. He is no longer unknown.

Notice the focus of this event is these 'stones.' These stones are for the next generations of God's people. See what it says, *"When your children ask…"* (Joshua 4:6). The 'children' here, are not just the children of those who came across the Jordan. See chapter 4:21 *"When your children ask their fathers in time to come saying What are these stones?"* *"…In Time to come…"* This pile of stones would be a sign for future generations. These stones have a significant purpose.

The purpose was to strike fear into the heart of their children, *"…that you may fear the Lord your God forever"* (Josh 4:24). How many children's books today produce a healthy fear of the Lord? "The beginning of wisdom?" The concept is that the continuity of the church is furthered by the fear of God. That's quite radical is it not? We spend so much time telling children God loves them but never tell them to fear Him. They just told a story that would strike fear into anybody who considered it. I wonder if so many children from believing homes would forsake the Lord if they had been given a healthy fear of Him throughout their lives. Should He not be feared?

The head of this work is ordinary fathers. Real men who have a wife and children and a job. They must teach their children in a particular way. This is the subject in this chapter at the very entrance to the Promised Land. These are principles set for all time by God for families. How did Israel keep the vision of a Promised Land? They were four hundred years in slavery, then forty years in the desert. How did they keep this vision?! The fear of the Lord was taught to children. The responsibility was firmly on the fathers. Joshua understood this. Pastor, dad, do you?

It is urgent that fathers take up their responsibility to ensure future generations of believers arise to propagate and teach the church of God. This is what Christian parenting is all about. That their children might learn early to pray, to read the scriptures, and understand something of divine power. To learn to recognize the hand of God in nature and in life on a day-to-day basis. Too many believing parents today are only concerned that their child finds a secure middle-class job. We need to change. The pastor or leader must have an aptitude to teach. He must have honed that aptitude by teaching his own children.

chapter sixty-six

BEING THE TEACHER

It is possible that many Christian men, experts in their professions, have never read a serious Christian book. They wouldn't know a Bible-believing publisher, nor the names of the great men of God from the past. They have never read any of the major confessions and couldn't teach a children's Bible class without a paid-for program, which they were unable to assess for its biblical accuracy. They read their Bible, but they show little serious interest in it or the things of God.

We should build such 'stones' into our family life. We might loosely call them family traditions, but traditions for the sake of traditions have never benefited the church. Some religious bodies are so full of tradition that the traditions themselves smother the life of the church. In the New Testament, traditions are glaring by their absence. Yet there are many ways to do this. The intention is to turn the conversation Godward. The church must have life and an experience of God today, to ratify the stones of the past.

Nature and life are replete with opportunities to talk about God and His salvation. In Joshua 4:19–20, they camped at Gilgal and Joshua took the stones and set them up there. The name 'Gilgal' means "circle of stones." And note finally on this point that Israel wouldn't be staying at Gilgal. They would be moving on from there to Jericho and beyond. Joshua's enemies were watching and listening and taking this activity in. It did soften their hard hearts, but only in the sense that it melted them with fear. Israel wasn't thinking about Jericho just yet. But Jericho was thinking about them.

SECTION XIV:
IS GOD FOR US OR AGAINST US?

chapter sixty-seven
CEREMONY BEFORE SERVICE

Joshua 5

At that time the Lord said to Joshua, "Make flint knives for yourself, and circumcise the sons of Israel again the second time." So Joshua made flint knives for himself, and circumcised the sons of Israel at the hill of the foreskins. ... Then the Lord said to Joshua, "This day I have rolled away the reproach of Egypt from you." Therefore the name of the place is called Gilgal to this day.
—Joshua 5:2–3, 9

Jericho was ripe for the taking. Yet rather than rush to take advantage of their weakness, Joshua took time to circumcise the men of Israel. This would weaken Israel physically for a few days. It appears that Joshua considered spiritual issues more important than winning battles. Joshua was acutely aware of who he was and who this nation was. He had a wonderful grasp of priorities. We must understand biblical priorities. These will guide us through many issues.

Joshua knew that the Lord would give him Jericho. But Joshua himself had to do something to create a defining moment for Israel. They still saw themselves as slaves and wanderers. They needed something to recreate them as God's people. As Abraham's children. Circumcision was that mark. They had ceased to be distinct. Neither slavery nor the wilderness wanderings made them lose their identity as God's people. However, in the desert, they didn't circumcise their children. They had been out of Egypt for forty years. The desert removed their identity as slaves, but their identity as God's people hadn't been fully restored. Here the Lord brings Israel back to base and gives them a new beginning, a fresh identification. Verse 9 says, *"Then the Lord said to Joshua, 'This day I have rolled away the reproach of Egypt from you.' Therefore the name of the place is called Gilgal to this day."*

Israel's identity was a physical mark. What is the New Testament believer's identity? How is it recognized? Is there something that sets us apart as different? I think the first observation to make is that from the mid-20th century until now, the church has been working frantically to rid itself of any distinctives. These were aspects both deep and superficial developed naturally over centuries. They are gone with few exceptions, and we are generally quite happy about that. Except that in some areas we "threw the baby out with the bathwater." In other areas, while not losing the essential (the baby), we lost some unifying features that kept us functioning smoothly as the universal church.

One example of this is that we no longer read the same Bible. Indeed, in any church today there will be many different translations. That would never be allowed in a university class on Shakespeare. Do more people in this liberated church read the Bible due to this upgrade? No, they don't. The proliferation of translations, one adding and subtracting, while the other subtracts and adds. They are no different theologically is the claim, but they are so different we can't read them together. We are a church that is identified by the curse of individualism... a poor replacement for the identity of the body of Christ.

Every church had an evangelistic service and a prayer meeting. Two of the most important aspects of the church's identity in the world. We have neither, and we don't miss either. We have few corporate views on biblical subjects. The church has lost its identity. The list is endless. To many of us, the church as it was known for centuries has ceased to exist.

Laying aside details and issues which we are free to differ on, the burning question is... are we a better church than those we pity and joke about? The answer is declared in the facts. The facts are condemning. Derisory attendance at prayer meetings. Most church members today have never led a soul to Christ. In a previous generation, most of us lost count before we were twenty. Worship, I love the modern worship songs. But they have served to confuse the unity of church worship. We no longer can go to a different church anywhere in the world and fully worship with the congregation. The exponential production of worship songs has made unified worship impossible. Well, money changes everything doesn't it?! Are we better off? No, we are not. Should we go back? Oh, please no!

The condemnation of the old church was that they got stuck in a rut they enjoyed. It became a grave. But we are no different, we are stuck in a rut of doing things because we can, without ever questioning the results. It is this writer's opinion that the present-day evangelical Bible-believing churches have lost their identity as the people of the Bible and the people of God. Nobody understands who we are. We don't understand ourselves anymore. Joshua saw this as a problem and fixed their identity before the battle.

Do you have a history that has identified you negatively? The Lord can turn it into a positive in a day. Not in any physical way but by an inward transformation, a new nature, a *"New Heart"* (Ezekiel 36:26)! He turns negatives into positives. Gilgal means "rolling." It is so named because here the Lord 'rolled' away the reproach, the shame of having no identity. This renewal accomplished, Joshua turned his mind to Jericho. Before Joshua deals with Jericho, God will deal with him. It is very necessary for every leader to make the discovery Joshua is about to make, and the sooner the better!

chapter sixty-eight

THE COMMANDER OF
THE ARMIES OF THE LORD

The few verses that deal with this next incident are given below. This is a unique insight into the life of Joshua. Joshua finds himself alone "*by Jericho.*" In all the years I have been reading this sentence, I get a consistent picture in my head. It has always just appeared in my head when I read this short account. Let me paint the picture...

When the Bible says "by" Jericho, I imagine Joshua at a vantage point overlooking the city surveying the task before him. This is what I see... A raised area of the lush, healthy landscape where Joshua has walked up and from which he can ponder, plan, and prepare for battle. It is a pensive moment for Joshua. A moment to ponder alone. Into that solitary moment, a man appears. A warrior. The exchange is brief between them but life-changing for Joshua. The lesson is essential for a balanced understanding of our relationship with God. It is given only a brief mention. Yet it is more important for Joshua than the taking of Jericho itself. Let's read the text first:

> *And it came to pass, when Joshua was by Jericho, that he lifted his eyes and looked, and behold, a Man stood opposite him with His sword drawn in His hand. And Joshua went to Him and said to Him, "Are You for us or for our adversaries?"*
>
> *So He said, "No, but as Commander of the army of the Lord I have now come."*

Being Joshua

And Joshua fell on his face to the earth and worshiped, and said to Him, "What does my Lord say to His servant?"

Then the Commander of the Lord's army said to Joshua, "Take your sandal off your foot, for the place where you stand is holy." And Joshua did so.

—Joshua 5:13–15

So... there Joshua is overlooking and thinking about Jericho. Although the things that have been done by Joshua to this point have had a larger focus than one city, this city was the first in Canaan. It must have seemed to Joshua that everything was ready. Joshua was as set as these stones to conquer the land. He had turned on his military expertise. A warrior already at war. So animated that he could assimilate an imaginary battle with a sweeping glance. Joshua was totally given to the moment.

The scripture uses a familiar phrase here. "*And it came to pass...*" Often the Bible uses such innocent phrases. They are not to be ignored. Here it introduces us to an atmosphere around Joshua. Joshua was in a particular place spiritually "*...by Jericho,*" a certain frame of mind. We might see it as a military consciousness. He was a seasoned soldier and a man of God. I imagine him stopping, seriously, battle-ready, alert, one knee posture, head bowed before God (he had to "*lift his eyes*"). Joshua was sensing the battle. His whole being embraced Jericho. The fight had started for Joshua. That's my picture of this moment "*By Jericho.*"

We are brought to a dead stop. We are as surprised as Joshua when we read the Bible saying "*...and behold, a man stood opposite him*" (Joshua 5:13). (The KJV more pertinently says, "*Against Him*"). The idea is instantly of a man in a position that was tense and potentially dangerous. Joshua knew all about posturing in fighting. This man is clearly a warrior—the sword drawn in his hand is just the fear confirmed. Yet, Joshua wasn't afraid. He demanded an answer to a concise question: "*Are you for us or for our adversaries?*" Joshua is ready to fight with this man, and he confronts him, whoever he is.

The Commander of the Armies of the Lord

On Joshua confronting him, Athanasius says this is the best way to go when confronted by an enemy… "The evil messengers cannot stand before a challenge; the good messengers respond with joy."[9] Confrontation has become a bad word, but it isn't necessarily bad. It needs only to be simple and straightforward, or so Joshua thought!

Joshua imagines that the moment will be controlled by his question. He intends this man to be controlled by his question. How often we ask God questions and don't realize that many of our questions are wrong to begin with! So here with Joshua.

---

9   Athanasius, *The Life of Antony Nicene and Post Nicene Fathers Vol. IV*, 208.

chapter sixty-nine
ARE YOU FOR US OR AGAINST US?

Joshua 5:13–15

We are told, "Joshua went to him." What a man is Joshua!? He is alone within sight of Jericho. There is a warrior ready before him. He is confronted by a significant warrior! Joshua isn't afraid. Then again, perhaps he should be. He knows the danger is life-threatening. From the narrative, the man is clearly a figure to be reckoned with. Yet Joshua isn't afraid. Again, note that perhaps he should be! He goes to him and confronts the man. Joshua has an equal in his mind—one warrior against another.

The conversation we are privy to is unique. A cautious Moses had this conversation at the burning bush in Exodus 3. A terrified Jacob had it in the desert fleeing from his brother in Genesis 28. Unbelieving Thomas had it in that room in John 20:27. Bewildered Saul had it on the Damascus Road. Here Joshua is about to have it. Yet Joshua is, unlike these examples, not afraid! Oh, how easily we adopt a posture in the presence of those we don't know! Joshua is clear-headed in his purpose. He needs to know one thing only about this man before he draws his sword and dispatches him. "*Are you for us or for our adversaries*" (verse 13)? Joshua isn't up for a conversation. He isn't about to negotiate. He assumes a taking of sides. A declaration of allegiance. How often the Lord's answers to our questions refuse to fit into our box! Often when we think we are clear-sighted we are in fact blind to the reality before us. We don't know Him! Joshua demands an answer on his terms. He demands that God answers: their side or our side? The "man" answers... with a blunt... "No"!

You will see how this answer is bewildering to Joshua. There are only two sides to be identified, which side are you on? *"No,"* says the man. *"But as commander of the army of the Lord I have now come"* (verse 14)! What a shock. See how God won't be drawn to our service, not be subjected to our concepts or our perceptions of reality. He remains holy, always. *That is, apart.* What is this army he refers to? Is Israel not the army of God? Yes, it is in human terms. This man commands heavenly armies!

God is never ours to own. He is never at our command. Even for Joshua, God remains in His own place. Joshua demonstrates how to respond. He falls on his face! He senses defeat before the battle has begun.

Joshua fell on his face. *God will win over us, before He will win for us.* "What does my Lord say to His servant?" Joshua was gearing up for a fight. God removed that fight from him. He is no longer in charge. He no longer carries the burden of this city. *"... the battle is not yours, but God's"* (2 Chron 20:15). A real blow has been delivered to Joshua. It has defeated him, yet it will strengthen him. His trust and confidence have been removed. He is again a servant... not a warrior. He fell on his face and worshipped! Now, Joshua's response needs further analysis.

chapter seventy

CHRIST IN ALL THE SCRIPTURES

In the book of Revelation when John the Apostle falls at the feet of the angel and worships, the angel says "...*See that you do not do that...*" (Rev 19:10)! We worship God alone. How is it then, that this personage offers no such rebuke? How is it that Joshua feels no discomfort in this prostrated position of worship? One answer satisfies here. Joshua realizes he is in the presence of divinity. Before we proceed... have you had this experience? Have you met God in a way that reduced you to humility, submission, and worship? Seek this moment if you desire to serve God.

The second person of the Trinity, like the third person in Old Testament times, waited for a day to come, when He would appear in a different way. God the Son, like God the Spirit, reveals Himself throughout the Old Testament in a rare and hidden manner. Joshua knew this in a veiled way. Surely, he had been taught this by his parents and certainly by his mentor Moses. Hence, Joshua senses the presence of divinity, of God the Son. This view is held by many throughout the history of the church. Calvin, in his commentary on Joshua, says clearly this was the Son of God.

Calvin's last literary work was written months before he died while in a state of extreme exhaustion and illness due to his strenuous work for the kingdom of God. In this condition, he wrote his commentary on the book of Joshua. He had been pressed by friends to write and by other friends to desist and retire. His response to these good and well-meaning friends was, "Would you that the Lord, when He comes, should find me idle!" Calvin's answer to the question of exactly what form He appeared in this moment with

Joshua is concluded with Calvin saying simply, "It is needless to discuss, as it seems wrong to insist upon any particular view on the subject"! Don't you just love Calvin?

However more interestingly, there is also a relevant quote from Origen in the Editorial Note on page 88. Here it points out that "…modern commentaries followed in the steps of the Jewish Rabbis who declared without evidence or support, that this angel was Michael. Calvin sides with the sounder view…" held by the early Christian Fathers, and "…which is well expressed by Origen who says in his sixth homily on the book of Joshua …" Joshua knew not only that he was of God, but that he was God. For who else is the Captain of the Lord's hosts but our Lord Jesus Christ?"[10]

Within sight of Jericho, Joshua is turned from warrior to worshipper. Never lose this priority. Joshua is turned from being ready to face up to anyone, to lying face down listening. With apparent speed he responds, *"What does my Lord say to His Servant?"* (Verse 14). Can anything be further from fighting, than this? Right now, we are privileged to see this event. To live through it with Joshua. To feel it is to covet it! Joshua is ready to take on Jericho, but God wants to reduce him to a "servant" first. How often have we seen this point in the story so far? Joshua gets it instantly… do you? This is the starting point for doing anything significant for God. It isn't an inspirational weekend's ministry or a special prayer meeting, it is the need to give evidence that you know who you are and who God is. The request was simple, "… *'Take your sandal off your foot, for the place where you stand is holy.' And Joshua did so"* (Josh 5:15). As a point of interest, The NKJV translates this singular "sandal" and "foot." Other translations bring the words into plural form, sandals and feet. The NKJV is true to the Hebrew word which is singular in both cases. To throw down one shoe was a statement of intention to invade a land, a sort of claim to ownership. Joshua was going to subdue Canaan. Hence Joshua is commanded to take of his 'shoe.'

---

10 *Calvin's Commentary, Vol IV, on the Book of Joshua,* Trans. Henry Beverage, (Grand Rapids, Michigan: Baker Book House), 88.

However, Joshua is also told the ground he stands upon is holy ground. This gives the impression that there is something spiritual going on, not necessarily tied to Jericho at all. But why then was Joshua told to take off one shoe? God's presence sets the space apart. Of this, there can be no debate. It is easy to understand the interest to make it plural, "Shoes off your feet" as other translations do. Holy ground doesn't want to be contaminated with the dust of this world. Also, Joshua isn't going to subdue Canaan, the Lord will do that. Joshua more than likely removed both shoes. Then again, in the context of Joshua on a war footing right by Jericho, perhaps a little less demand is placed upon him.

"What does my Lord say to His Servant?" The idea that we are this level of servant is a great challenge. It is too much to ask, too high a standard. We have inverted the order. Joshua may have been guilty because the Lord had to return him to basics before he was of any use at Jericho. We can be guilty of treating God as though He is our servant. We make constant demands just like Joshua did. All couched in submissive language, but all looking for God to do something for us, or our friend. "Are you for us or against us" represents many prayers at prayer meetings. It is our turn to be asked by the Lord, "Are you for us or against us?" If you are… fall on your face and take your shoes off your feet. Find within your heart Joshua's response: *"…What does my Lord say to His servant?"*

SECTION XV:
UNDERSTANDING DEVOTED TO DESTRUCTION

chapter seventy-one

JERICHO, AN ASSESSMENT

Joshua Chapter 6:1

So much is contained about Joshua and Jericho in these first few words: *"Now Jericho was securely shut up..."* (Joshua 6:1). The picture is of a city on lock-down. The text expands the situation, in case we don't quite get it, *"...none went out, and none came in"* (Joshua 6:1). The armies of Israel were probably sitting within eyesight. War was in the air.

The population was terrified, the rulers were in hiding. They had no heart for war with an army commanded by God. They were even afraid of this man called Joshua. The earlier spies reported giants and warriors of repute: a terrifying, efficient fighting machine. They also reported their evil and vile culture. They were too powerful a nation to defeat. But forty years later we aren't reading about giants, warriors, or great armies. They are so out of shape they are no longer a terror; they are terrified. Their soldiering is collecting a wage, not waging war.

God had blessed Canaan. He had particularly blessed Jericho and made it great. They thought they had done it themselves, but it was the Lord—He gave them abundant harvests while Israel ate Manna. They had food of every sort in abundance. God's goodness was supposed to bring them to repentance. Paul describes this in Romans:

> *Or do you despise the riches of His goodness, forbearance, and long-suffering, not knowing that the goodness of God leads you to repentance? But in accordance with your*

> *hardness and your impenitent heart you are treasuring up for yourself wrath in the day of wrath and revelation of the righteous judgment of God.*
>
> —Romans 2:4–5

Repentance wasn't on Jericho's agenda. They had just become vile sloths. They didn't turn to Him like Nineveh did. Even now, with certain defeat and death imminent, they couldn't find it in themselves to repent. Sin so hardens us that even when we know that repentance is needed, we can't stir it in our hearts.

These are universal principles of our fallen world. Ancients often recognized them. Many an old man cursed sin while looking back over a ruined life. Many grandmothers warned their granddaughters to recognize the signs of fallen nature, the signs of a man governed by mere sinful passions. But the granddaughters of Jericho were as corrupt as the grandfathers. The poor man in the street had the same connoisseur-like taste for evil as the rich. Sin destroys men's vitals.

Jericho had been living on past success for decades. The leaders and soldiers knew how to talk about war and look strong, but their armour was dull, their swords were blunt. The rippling muscles that earned them esteem were flabby. The only thing that was still much alive was their appetite for sin, which was never satisfied. As they practiced in their courtyards, they would discover that their favourite moves and skills were rusty. Their best leaders were drunk by lunchtime, and the city was awash with filth. They could of course still 'bluster,' huff and puff and posture on these wobbly Jericho walls.

Learn the signs of spiritual slippage. The church can become like this… empty talk, self-delusion, dead traditions, and dishonesty, resembling a religious Jericho. Pastors, examine your appetites! Listen to your sermons and examine your words! Examine your expectations. Many of our sermons are mere hustle and bustle. Church member, when did your heart last stir at the name of Jesus? When did you last repent?

chapter seventy-two

JERICHO... SHUT UP!

Joshua 6:1 tells us pertinently "... *Jericho was securely shut up.*" This phrase might indicate secure battlements, high walls, and great doors—an impenetrable city. These walls were built when Jericho was at the height of its success. However, the inhabitants couldn't have confidence in this picture. They knew the walls were in decay, and... the Jordan stopped at Adam.

Indulgence suffocates diligence. Jericho was shut up in more ways than militarily. Yes, the city officials had shut the doors. But it was God that had shut Jericho up. The meaning of "Jericho" isn't clear. Some say it means "fragrance."[11] But it was an evil 'fragrance' that Jericho spread throughout Canaan. Evil is difficult to contain. Hence Jericho was securely shut up!

Jericho had been living with its doors open, unafraid of anyone. All the cities were the same. Nobody around was going to attack. Everybody milked the wealth and resources of Jericho. But God wasn't happy with Jericho! You understand that we can have all the people around us saying we are great. But it's what God thinks that we need to hear. The Bible says, "... *God is angry with the wicked every day*" (Psalm 7:11). God had observed as Jericho spilled evil into the surrounding countryside. Every hill and dale, every mountain and glen fouled by their speech and behaviour. Every green tree and hedgerow, stained by their evil practices.

---

11 Robert Young, *Analytical Concordance to the Whole Bible* (London: Lutterworth Press, 1879), 537.

The poor, while they partook of the evil, also suffered the indulgence of the rich. When the city spilled over into the countryside, men ran and hid. They took their children and barricaded them. The cry was "the city is coming!" This cry may have been expressed variously. It may only have been a start in a mother's heart. But it ruined many and was a scourge on the land. But since Israel crossed the Jordan, the countryside began to sense pleasant silence… Jericho was securely "shut up"!

Many a quiet evening in an orchard or on a farm would have been shattered by the raucous cries of the partygoers from Jericho. Invading, plundering, vandalizing days of hard labour. Young men who answered to nobody would surge out and plunder… but not tonight! The night air would be filled with the jarring noise of the city, that incessant hum and cry would spill out sending nature's chorus far away… but not tonight! Had Jericho used this restraint and repented, the land might have recovered. As the doors closed, the siren's lure slipped into silence. Tonight, parents slept peacefully because… Jericho was shut up! This was the effect of the Old Testament church on both the city and the land of Canaan. Is your church influencing your community?

Did the inhabitants wonder if something good was about to happen? The judgement of God benefits the world more than it hurts. Men learn righteousness. Oh, that God would shut our cities up like Jericho and silence their practices and their profanities. Close their doors, shut their blinds, barricade them inside their caverns like bats, and let real people get on with their legitimate lives. The book of Joshua, were it to be made into a movie, could well be called *Jericho… Shut Up!* This is precisely what God was going to do throughout Canaan beginning with Jericho. He intended to shut down wickedness and plant righteousness. In verse 2 the Lord tells Joshua, "… *See I have given Jericho into your hand, its king and the mighty men of valor.*" Yet Jericho saw themselves differently. They thought they were secure! They thought nobody could get in. Sadly, they had no desire to get out! They were pitiless and deserving of the coming judgement.

chapter seventy-three

THE ART OF WAR

Joshua 6:3.

As soon as Jericho was secured, and note they had shut themselves in, God began to instruct Joshua on the procedures to follow to win this battle. Again, please note that an army taking a city wasn't a new idea. Battle procedures were well established and most armies knew what to do in any given set of circumstances. One of the most famous war manuals is the ancient Chinese manual, *The Art of War*. It has been dated variously 5,000–3,000 BC. A long time before Joshua. Sometimes we wonder, do men know anything else but the art of war?

Joshua had been a soldier for forty years. He still understood that his call was to do what God tells him, not what his experience tells him. The Lord was fighting this battle and He is the commander of the Lord's armies that will do the fighting! Joshua listened. He is told to march around the city once a day for six days with all the armed men. Then he is told to make seven priests carry trumpets of rams' horns in front of the Ark; they are to sound the trumpets before the Ark, but the people must stay quiet every day until Joshua tells them to "shout!" On the seventh day, they must march around the city seven times, with the priests blowing the trumpets. When they hear a long blast on the trumpets, all the people are told to give a loud shout; then the walls of the city would collapse and the people would go up, everyone straight in. They did this as commanded. The soldiers were silent until the command to shout was given.

Now, this procedure had no foundation in any art of war. This was utterly pointless to the onlookers. If anything, the warriors of Jericho by the third day were beginning to get their confidence back. The behaviour they were watching was fantasy! Of course, the superstitious might imagine some dark magic was being processed. Nobody in Jericho understood. Nobody in Israel understood. God understands!

Now ask yourself, what were they doing?! What was so powerful about this action? What kind of confidence expected Jericho's doors to fall off, let along their walls to collapse, by merely walking in circles?! If you had been there, what would you have said? Joshua wasn't the only experienced warrior. They had all fought battles in the desert. What would they have been saying? Well, we don't know. They were told to say nothing, but in their hearts and minds… what was going on? It is arguable from the outcome that they were believing God would keep His word! This whole army was filled with faith. A vision to behold. A whole congregation filled with active faith. Can you imagine the effect of such a church? *"But without faith it is impossible to please Him, for he who comes to God must believe that He is, and that He is a rewarder of those who diligently seek Him"* (Hebrews 11:6).

What do we know? Well, we know that Joshua was told in advance the walls would fall. We know they did fall, as predicted. We know that Israel obeyed to the letter. We know they expected victory because God was with them. The only answer, therefore, is that Israel believed God! Faith was their victory. *"… this is the victory that overcomes the world—our faith"* (1 John 5:4). So, is there evidence of faith in your life? Is that faith active? Have you seen 'walls' fall down? What are your expectations for church life? Do you realize that the Lord sends tests for our faith regularly and particularly before significant moments? He does this to reset our vision of Him as God and fix our faith afresh upon Him. Jordan was the test to get Israel into the right place with Him before Jericho.

chapter seventy-four
UNDERSTANDING DEVOTION

Joshua 6 verses 6–25 records the actual event: the marching around, the silence, the trumpets sounding, and the seventh day with that final blast and the walls falling. The soldiers attacked and Rahab the harlot was saved with her entire family. Note an interesting word that needs explanation in verse 17. In the New International Version, it says *"The city and all that is in it are to be devoted to the Lord..."* (Joshua 6:17, NIV). Most translations change this. For example: "... *doomed by the Lord to destruction*" (NKJV); "... *devoted to the Lord for destruction*" (ESV). While the NKJV is my preferred text, in this instance the ESV seems to have the most comprehensive grasp using "devoted" and "destruction" together. A strange combination.

The bare word "devoted" jars the modern ear. Devotion and destruction don't sit well together because our idea of "devotion" presents warmth. There is no image of destruction in 'devotion.' The word has become weak, almost insipid—just a nice word, meaning love and worship. It demands nothing and produces nothing. However, the real meaning is more like sterilizing—cleansing, purifying. These are words that kill and burn germs.

'Devoting' means to purify and set apart. The 'destruction' provided purification. The whole event was an offering to God, purifying Canaan by purging it of evil. They didn't repent, and Jericho was thoroughly 'devoted' to the Lord. Our understanding is aided by both words being used together.

The God revealed in the Old Testament scriptures is thoroughly holy. We must grasp this understanding again. It might restrain our party idea of worship. Our musicians and worshippers might have a little more revision, examination, and preparation, in their exercise of "*devotion*" to the Lord. Worship isn't just deep gratitude. It is a separation from sin and all that is unholy.

chapter seventy-five
SAVED AMIDST DESTRUCTION

The walls of Jericho fell flat. These great walls that wicked Jericho trusted in for safety were destroyed—not merely by men sounding trumpets, but by God's invisible armies, their commander, the second person of the trinity. Joshua and the armies of Israel simply watched as they fell. A great cloud of dust was sufficient to smother Jericho's hollow posturing; they probably mocked God's people as they marched day by day. Not the first morning. That first morning their hearts melted. They were afraid. They hadn't slept. They were on the wall before daylight, nervously awaiting the onslaught and the possibility of death. But by the third day, they began to make jokes about Israel's weird tactics. They slept late. On the fourth morning, I muse, they were startled into heavy-eyed wakening by the trumpets at dawn... I muse... that night they drank themselves into a drunken stupor. They didn't hear the trumpets on the fifth morning. When they stirred and nursed themselves, Israel had been and gone... that was their waking dream... they have gone! For a day they thought Israel hadn't walked round. Perhaps Israel changed their mind, decided against attack. Perhaps Israel had realized they couldn't succeed. But they heard the trumpets on the sixth morning and ushered the return of their terror. They calmed one another with flimsy imaginations of victory. By the dark evening of the sixth day (I am imagining...) They were lifting their spirits, shouting empty threats into the night from the walls; Israel was relaxed, having supper, and waiting upon God. Tomorrow was coming.

The warriors of Jericho were convincing themselves that Israel had fled the scene. Surely the quiet night told them all was well—until the sun spread a great light over the plains of Moab and lit up the walls. The created world gazed upon their grandeur... for the last time... It started early that day. A deep, rhythmic thudding began outside.

Jericho rose and went to the walls. The first trumpet blast brought an awakening shudder... a change to the pattern! They scrambled to find a bow, a sword, a flimsy leather shield, some bent arrows, anything that they could find—they weren't prepared for this moment. Something far down in the memory banks of these ancient warriors told them this is different! Before they could alert their comrades, a seismic shudder shook them to their core. They grasped and stumbled like the drunken fools they were, called out to one another for help, and old warriors dropped their spears and weapons trying vainly to find a firm foundation. Back and forth they swayed as mortar and stone began to shake and disintegrate around them. They looked to the left and to the right to engage the enemy... only to bump and crash into their fellows. The odd, still stubborn sinner managed to shoot off an arrow. It went nowhere. He called his fellows to muster. He found a trumpet of his own. Standing upright on the grinding, collapsing wall that was his trust, he pressed it to his lips and blew hard as he could into the cool morning sky, but it just spat dust and squeaked, it was out of shape like he was. He grabbed his sword handle and wrenched it out of its scabbard. Only the handle came, the blade stuck by rust. He fell on his stiff knees, to his hands, and there cried out to his gods for mercy, assuring the wrong god of devotion. If he could but live out this day he would change... But his dumb, stone deity returned no answer, not even a change of expression. It disappeared into the crumbling rocks as did the once-great warrior. He lived without God and died alone in judgement. Few tried to run backwards to get off the wall into the city but were thrown into the charge of the Israelites as the walls of Jericho fell... outwards! This was the morning of the seventh day. The number of completion. Here on the seventh day, God's dealings with Jericho would be complete. Israel would walk onto the great city over the pile of rubble that yesterday was great walls.

It took what seemed like no time at all for these great walls to completely fall flat. Silence would have been a respite, but the armies of Israel had a work of devotion to accomplish, and that they did. Before the midday sun released its full heat, Jericho was 'devoted.' Nature sighed a sad, peaceful sigh.

The world around began to emerge, to walk freely, to laugh again, to play, to plant and to build. Something was gone... fear and filth were gone. The air was clean. Family and friendship, and above all righteousness, gently ruled again. What was once the environs of the great evil machine called the city, was flattened to a mere mound. Its gates would no longer open to scourge the world. Jericho was devoted to destruction.

But Rahab was saved from the same.

chapter seventy-six
THEOLOGICAL HISTORY

Think about Rahab. Why don't we see further questions about the two spies? This reflects the principle that new emergencies supersede the previous; yesterday's disaster is shelved in favour of today's, even if it was a matter of national security. Politicians work this mentality to their profit. Jericho conveniently forgot Rahab, but she didn't forget. Nor had she been forgotten.

It's timely now to take a step back and ask: what is this book of Joshua about? We haven't quite looked at six full chapters. Yet we have moved through significant major subjects. Having tasted the book, we might be able to answer: 'What is this book about?' In the first six chapters, Israel has a significant leadership change. The book of Joshua begins with a moment of sober change. When significant men die, the tension is palpable. Moses died and Joshua took the reins. Yet the book isn't about dynasties as such. Is it about Joshua? In terms of the new leadership, it is. However, Joshua isn't front and centre of the narrative or the main speaker. The main speaker is the Lord.

The first nine verses, half of the first chapter, are a transcript of what God said to Joshua! The Lord spoke about how He would stand by Joshua in taking Canaan. The second half of chapter one is an important, but seemingly secondary, issue, the request of the two-and-a-half tribes to settle on the other side of Jordan and their promise to fight until Canaan was conquered. A mere technicality, caution regarding a contract, is almost a letdown after the glorious commitment God made to Joshua.

Chapter two gets quickly on to the subject we expected, warfare... spies! But we might notice this isn't the main point of the narrative. Only half of the first verse tells us about spying. We are told they found a good place to hide in Jericho. The following twenty-one of the twenty-four verses in chapter two talk about Rahab... a prostitute! What's going on here? Historical records? Surely, but something else as well.

In the enticing first few chapters of the book of Joshua, we are reading not about great generals or the achievements of men, but about God and a sinful woman in a sinful city who lived on the wall. How does the story evolve? In chapter three, a historical account would be about how engineers forded a river. There is no record of any engineering or anything about men at all—except priests. That's what we read in this historical account. Priests take on the first great challenge of Canaan, the crossing of Jordan. All they do is stand in the water... it is a profoundly religious event. The book of Joshua is profound, religious history.

Religious matters have been part of the history of every nation. Many nations are embarrassed by their religious history. More are ashamed of their religion and its history. The current religious history of the West is strange. While officially rejecting the belief in God, we still maintain religion as fundamentally useful. Atheism is always contradictory.

Joshua is placed with similar books: Judges, Ruth, Samuel, Kings, Chronicles, Ezra Nehemiah, and Esther. This we call the 'historical' section of the Bible. These are historical accounts of ancient Israel. They contain records of events, people, and places. However, other significant things happen in history as well as wars and disasters. The Bible, from beginning to end, is the story of God's revelation of Himself and the salvation He provided for us in Jesus Christ. We used to call it His-story! It's much more exciting and edifying. It's glorious.

chapter seventy-seven

BEING THE ONLY GOOD THING IN JERICHO

Rahab had clearly become a believer. James says, "*... was not Rahab the harlot also justified by works when she received the messengers and sent them out another way?*" (James 2:25). James argues that faith is evidenced by works. Works are both the natural and the necessary result of real faith. "*For as the body without the spirit is dead, so faith without works is dead also*" (James 2 26). Works aren't a contributor to salvation; they are a natural result of salvation. James isn't saying Rahab's good works saved her, he is saying her good works were evidence of true faith.

Matthew Henry says "Such a faith set her above the fear of man, even the wrath of the king. She believed, upon the report she had heard of the wonders wrought for Israel, that their God was the only true God..."[12] She had met God's servants and found them to be honourable men. Maybe they were the first such men she had met! She had heard of and seen the power of the God of Israel. In this passage, she and her family are being taken to safety by Joshua's young men. They now have a future and a hope. It may be said that Rahab was the only good in Jericho. This new convert won her whole family to faith in God. That is real evidence of salvation. But what of all the detail? What place does the flax have or the scarlet cord? What is the point of all the conversational details? Well, they certainly substantiate it as an accurate report. The detail is one of the marks of a real conversation. Details tell us things. The level of

---

12 Matthew Henry, *Matthew Henry's Commentary on the Whole Bible* (Hendrickson Publishers, 1992), 7.

detail in the story of Rahab supports the case as real history; it also shows that we are reading theological history.

chapter seventy-eight

GOD REVEALS HIMSELF TO US

God reveals Himself to us in the Bible. In the book of Joshua, God is revealed as a God who wants to save us from the destruction of judgement. He promises to do this if we will put our trust in His Son. The Bible narrative takes us from creation and the fall to Christ and redemption, and on to heaven and God Himself. Joshua is a part of this story of God revealing Himself to the world as a God who saves. When we read the Old Testament, we should read it with this understanding. The ordinary reader who comes to the Bible, as I did, with no background, will quickly recognize that this is the story of the Bible. Where does Joshua fit in?

God had spoken to Abraham promising him a family and a land. The land was Canaan; the family, descendants of his grandson Jacob, whose name was changed to Israel. Israel had twelve sons who became the heads of the families of Israel. After four hundred years of slavery, God delivered them out of Egypt, and he carried them through the wilderness to the land promised to Abraham. That promise is fulfilled here in the book of Joshua. So, when we read about 'Joshua,' we are reading about more than the history of a nation. We read the story of God's promises being fulfilled. In the book, we see details, like flax and red chords, as I have mentioned. But these details often overshadow the characters and events. They relate to the history of salvation! Rahab herself, her flax, the scarlet cord of the spies, these are among the significant details that point us to Christ Himself.

SECTION XVI: FOUR WORDS FOR "PRESENCE"

chapter seventy-nine

BEING FAMOUS

Closing verses of chapter 6

"Then Joshua charged them at that time, saying, 'Cursed be the man before the Lord who rises up and builds this city Jericho…'"
—Joshua 6:26

Verse 27 tells us *"So the Lord was with Joshua, and his fame spread throughout all the country."*

God was clearly with Joshua as He was with Moses. The people obeyed him like they said they would. God brought him over the Jordan and fought for him defeating Jericho. Joshua and the people obeyed the commands of the Lord to the letter and followed the preparatory religious rites and practices. They launched out in faith to step into the Jordan and march around Jericho in silent obedience. God sent the Commander of His armies to fight for them at Jericho. Invisible angelic warriors fought alongside the humble Israelites. With the battle over, Joshua shoots to stardom in the ancient world of Canaan. His 'fame' spread throughout the country, a household name. Women and children and warrior statesmen, politicians and kings, all chatting about Joshua: a new warrior with a divine army at his disposal; well, although they aren't at his disposal, the heathen never understand. Joshua must have had a certain earned satisfaction—as a warrior and a leader of the people of God, he had won. We read the fulfillment of God's promise—they are in the Promised Land. God will always fulfill His word.

chapter eighty
BEING A TRESPASSER

Chapter 7

To grasp what is happening, we need to be reminded of the Lord's commands regarding the taking of Jericho, as found in chapter 6:18: *"... abstain from the accursed things, lest you become accursed when you take of the accursed things, and make the camp of Israel a curse, and trouble it."* This one verse may easily be passed over. However, it determines all that happens in chapter 7.

As Joshua is beginning to relax into his great victory, a shock is awaiting him. The shock is transmitted to us as we begin to read chapter 7: *"But..."*! The first word in the chapter is foreboding... things may not be as they appear! Language can be so powerful. One word can lift us to the highest heavens and reduce us to despair. Famous Joshua is about to be so reduced. In verse one, we are informed of a problem Joshua knows nothing about.

"But the children of Israel committed a trespass regarding the accursed things" (Joshua 7:1). We know, but Joshua does not. The word "accursed" is also translated as "devoted." You will remember the interesting use of "devoted"—something set apart for, or by, God. In the case of Jericho, everything unless otherwise specified, was to be destroyed.

The children of Israel had committed a trespass. "Trespass" is another interesting word. It's often translated simply as "sin," the generic word for wrongdoing. Three words could be used to sum up the English word 'sin.' These are 'sin,' 'trespass,' and 'iniquity.' They all mean wrongdoing, but they have specific wrongdoing in mind.

First: sin is, as I have said, generic. It means all the things we do that are wrong.

Second: trespass is more specific. It's the word meaning to cross a boundary. Here we have another easily understood term. It means to go too far. It only qualifies the sin in as much as the line is crossed. How far you have gone isn't the immediate concern of this word. It is only concerned with the fact… you crossed a line you were told not to cross.

Third: iniquity is perhaps the worst kind of sin. It means distortion, twisting out of shape. Like a plastic cup on a hot plate distorted by the heat. The cup can still function, but it is unreliable, and perhaps more pertinently, a beautiful thing has become ugly. The word of interest in this narrative is 'trespass.'

So, trespass in common parlance is like this: if I am doing fifty-one kilometres per hour and you are doing ninety-one kilometres per hour, and the speed limit is fifty, both of us are trespassing. Both of us are sinners; we went over a line; we committed a trespass. The human consciousness, since Adam, wants to cry out, "But you are worse than me," or "I am not as bad as him!" Of course, the ultimate deflection is to blame someone else. Adam said to God *"The woman whom You gave to be with me, she gave me of the tree, and I ate"* (Gen. 3:12). We hold a comparative value of trespassing. God doesn't view trespasses comparatively. God is dealing with the fact… both are guilty; both are sinners. Hence, Romans 3:23: *"… for all have sinned and fall short of the glory of God,"* and Romans 3:10: *"As it is written: 'There is none righteous, no, not one…'"* Although God does take note of differentials in sin (the murderer is worse than the thief), both are still sinners in the eyes of God. The comparison is of more interest to us, in as much as one hurts one person more than the other. However, both are condemning offences to God the judge.

chapter eighty-one

GOD BEING ANGRY

In Joshua 7:1, Israel is said to have committed a trespass regarding the devoted things. Then we are told the details, unknown by Joshua. Achan took of the accursed things: the anger of the Lord burned against Israel. Joshua was basking in fame. No indication is given in the narrative that Joshua sensed anything wrong at all. Neither is any indication given that Joshua was in any error. Beware, church leader, when everything seems to be just great!

The Bible quietly tells us what happened and then the secret reality: *"The anger of the Lord burned against the children of Israel"*! There are just a few short verses to read without a lot of time between them. But a significant distance in terms of relationship... and Joshua and Israel knew nothing... This is worth consideration for the modern church.

Sometimes we think we know everything going on in our church. If we find such a moment, we know the expert to call! But there are lots of surprises in life. "Things" don't necessarily go as they should. The abusive youth worker. Division in the oversight. The prominent family about to disintegrate. The staff member who commits a crime! The deliberate scheme to bring down a pastor. The list of surprises is endless. The biblical narrative illustrates the distance between fame and failure can be short. Pastors must walk cautiously in times of success.

Achan took '*accursed things*,' things 'devoted' to destruction. Nobody was around. He took them away and hid them. Achan took a Babylonish garment. They had forty years of desert living with the same clothes: *"Your garments did not wear out on you..."* (Deut

8:4). But they were hardly dressed like the Babylonians. One might have thought waiting another few years would be ok! But Achan couldn't even wait a few days! He couldn't resist the thought of looking good.

A wedge of gold. Achan had never had such a thing. But he didn't need to buy a house in Canaan. They would inherit houses and gardens and olive groves... freely given from God.

Covetousness infects our rational faculties. Hear the words of John in the New Testament: *"For all that is in the world—the lust of the flesh, the lust of the eyes, and the pride of life—is not of the Father but is of the world"* (1 John 2:16).

Only Achan knew of his actions, but observe the infection of this man's sin and the consequences as the story unfolds. In the first verse of chapter 7, we read: *"...Israel committed a trespass..."*! The whole nation is held accountable.

chapter eighty-two
PRESENCE BEING FOUR WORDS

It is hard to keep secrets. Especially from God! He is Omnipresent. Theological words embody rich definitions. Hear Herman Bavinck the Dutch theologian in his book *The Doctrine of God*: *"...He (God) fills heaven and earth; no one can be hid from his presence; He is a God at hand, and also afar off,"* (Jer 23:23,24; Ps139:7-10; Acts 17:2;) *"In him we live and move, and have our being"* (Acts 17:28).[13]

This attribute, omnipresence, simply means that God is everywhere all the time and that he isn't merely part of things. That is, God isn't a tree or in a tree, and He can't be 'contained' by anything. When we think of God's presence we tend to think in human terms. We should be thinking in spiritual terms. Every believer wants to know God's presence in daily experience. The Bible speaks of this presence using four distinct words. These are: 'proximity,' 'face,' 'countenance,' and 'fully.' Achan had forgotten this divine attribute and its component parts. Let's look at them before moving on.

The first is "proximity," the idea of being in the same place. See Moses just out of Egypt. Moses didn't want God to just *send them*, he wanted God to *go with them* to Canaan: *"... If Your Presence does not go with us, do not bring us up from here"* (Exodus 33:15). Similarly, listen to the Lord assuring Joshua of His presence as he takes over from Moses: *"...as I was With Moses, so I will be with you. I will not leave you nor forsake you"* (Josh 1:5). *"... for the*

---

13 Herman Bavinck, *The Doctrine of God*, trans. William Hendrickson (Edinburgh Scotland: Banner of Truth Trust, 1979), 157.

Lord your God is with you wherever you go" (Josh 1:9). *"...the living God is among you"* (Josh 3:10). These texts infer God's presence in terms of 'proximity,' God being in the same place as us, with us.

The second word used to describe God's presence is "face." Psalm 27:8 says, *"When you said, "Seek my face," My heart said to You, Your face, Lord, will I seek."* Here is a proximity that is close enough to see the other person's face! Much closer than just general proximity. We often feel the need to see God with eyes of faith. To know Him better than just a fellow traveller. We want to be close enough to see His face shining upon us.

The third word is a particularly precious word, a beautiful concept. The word is "countenance." This is where the Bible gets incisive. In my first book, *Being Joseph*, I commented on Joseph when he sees the butler and the baker one morning and says to them "Why are you so sad?" The question I raised in the book is... how did Joseph know they were sad? Because they were in prison? Yes, but many prisoners aren't miserable every day. They sometimes laugh and chat cheerfully. But this morning Joseph saw something different... He saw their countenance. It had changed. Joseph knew these two men enough to have become familiar. So familiar that he could read their emotional state.

Can you tell when God is pleased? Or more to the text, when He is angry? That is the level of relational closeness that God invites his people to have with Him. He is so present that He sees into our hearts and minds. He wants to reveal Himself to us in love, more than we can even imagine.

The fourth word is slightly less obvious. It is the word "fully." Jude uses this word in his letter: *"Now to Him who is able to keep you from stumbling, and to present you faultless before the presence of His glory with exceeding joy..."* (Jude 1:24). The Greek word Katenopion is the word for presence used here. It has the sense of 'being fully in His presence.' Many are happy with God's presence in their proximity. Fewer are those who have the joy of seeing His face! Fewer still can recognize his countenance. Those fully in His presence are in heaven, but the aim while on earth is to have a taste of heaven and so to seek this level of God's presence. The Lord's table would be a good place to be fully in His presence. But the privacy of our own devotions is where we might occasionally experience Him in a measured sense of this word 'fully.' This never becomes ours to keep or control. He is God, and He determines our experience based on His analysis. His willingness to reveal Himself to us is never to be doubted, but it will be qualified by our exercise of faith and His analysis of where we are in Him.

So back to Achan! Achan was happy that God's presence was with Israel. How else could they defeat the great city, Jericho? He wasn't interested in any other level of presence. What he failed to realize is that God was still present... God is still here, caring for us, watching over us protecting, and providing for us, even if we have shut him out. He was there in that war-torn house in Jericho when Achan took the things devoted to destruction. Even God's presence in terms of mere proximity is potent. But His countenance was angry.

chapter eighty-three

WE ARE NEVER ALONE

Achan had missed this expectation! He somehow imagined he was a solitary figure in Jericho when forty thousand warriors came up against the city. He didn't recognize that there was an unseen army of angelic warriors commanded by the Son of God all around him, fighting for him and the rest of Israel. Because Achan couldn't see his fellows around him, he assumed he was alone, isolated enough to sin with impunity. Much worse... he didn't believe that God was omnipresent. He didn't feel His presence. But Achan was on God's 'watch list,' and he would soon sense His anger.

Achan believed that it was God who was isolated! He believed that God was far away, restricted, stuck in heaven. God might be somewhere, but not where Achan was. So, he took the accursed thing, dreamily convinced nobody knew. But right then, as he put it in his tunic, the angelic warriors gasped at his brazen betrayal. The gold wedge was 'devoted' for destruction, yet Achan tucked it away, devoting it for himself! Unbelief blinds us to spiritual realities that are about to become physical. This travesty was occurring, and Joshua still didn't know.

So, church leaders and pastors need to remember this as a reality. God is with us, even when we might wish he was not! Believers still sin, sometimes with impunity, but always in his presence! Think about that.

God knows our sins. His commander, and the legions of angelic warriors, saw Achan. Achan alone was highlighted among the forty thousand Israelites. He stood out as shockingly bad in the spiritual realm. Soon, he would stand out among men as well. Our grasp of truth should affect our daily living. When sound biblical theology doesn't produce practice, something has failed. Generally, it is us. God is with us, and our daily manner of life should demonstrate that. True faith includes this sort of thinking. Everything we do is done in full view of the Lord Jesus. We are 'yoked' together (Matt 11:28). Consider this when imagining sin is a 'secret.' Joshua was learning, always learning. Pastor, elder, church leader, remember, *God is always with you, even when it doesn't feel like it*. This truth is most often beneficial and pleasant. Here it is a cautionary tale.

chapter eighty-four
BEING JUST A LITTLE TOWN

And so, the story continues, and Joshua sends spies to the town of Ai. The spies said, "... *the people of Ai are few*" (Josh 7: 3). It was beside Beth Aven, on the east side of Bethel. Beth Aven means 'The house of vanity.' Bethel means 'The house of God.' What a picture the Bible paints in a few names. Achan was spiritually in this place, halfway between the house of God and ruin. This 'halfway' place isn't a tipping point. It isn't a fulcrum, it's a one-way street, and Achan was going in the wrong direction. Note the biblical estimate of fashion... a vain thing that can ruin you. There are situations where we are at a point of decision, and it could go either way. This isn't such a place. Achan decided at Jericho, and now he was on the way to ruin.

It was absolutely just a little town! The spies were right. It is estimated that Ai only had around twelve thousand inhabitants.[14] Hence the spies recommended two or three thousand men be sent. Joshua sent the higher number. Nobody knew the problem awaiting them was right in their midst... Achan. Achan was one of the three thousand chosen to go to Ai. Thirty-six men were killed, and Israel was put to flight by this little town! You may remember this phrase from Rahab's conversation with the spies: "... *our hearts melted...*" Here the same emotional terror is repeated, but this time it is the hearts of the people of God that "melt." What a fall! From Jordan,

---

14 Merrill Tenney, Zondervan's Bible Dictionary (Grand Rapids, Michigan: Zondervan, 1967), 26.

from Jericho, to tiny little Ai. Ai was merely the catalyst God used to bring them to their knees.

God can work wonders in us when we are humbled and afraid. We benefit from this if we respond well. Joshua responded well. *"Joshua tore his clothes and fell to the earth before the ark of the Lord until evening..."* (Joshua 7: 6). This is the mark of a man of God. Not looking initially for a cause, not instantly seeking to apportion blame. Rather, he is experiencing the moment. Not regarding himself, but how it affected God's people. He didn't get angry. He reacted personally but carried the elders in his response before God. His trusted elders joined him in repentance, humbling themselves before God. They did this for a whole day until the evening came. Evening is a wonderful portion of the day. Many good decisions are made in the evening, after a day of meditative thought... *Never rush to judgement.*

chapter eighty-five
BEING QUIET BEFORE JUDGEMENT

Can we discover Joshua's inner motives? Can we discover his thinking? How often do we react to an emotional spike and hustle and bustle and break things in pointless rage? Venting, we call it, opening a valve to release steam to reduce pressure. This merely increases things, spreading it to everyone around, drawing others into our turmoil, a multiplication of mess.

Not Joshua and the elders of Israel. They quietly waited upon God.

And nobody knew what was wrong, if anything! Learn from Joshua. In an earlier day, he had to learn this control. He learned in the difficulties of life to sit quietly in God's presence and let everything simmer and settle. Let the emotions calm, let the multitude of words be discovered, exposed in the silence, as 'empty.' Let them go, they are useless. Angry men use words that are vacuous. Learn to leave them where they are, undisturbed, before they arise and disturb. This doesn't mean that we simply let everything go to find peace. There is no lasting peace in unreality. I wonder if Joshua learned this in Egypt when he was unable to intervene as a slave. In Egypt, the young Joshua could only sit quietly in the presence of God and hear His calming counsel. In that powerless place, he gained a heavenly perspective on every pain. Perhaps Joshua the slave learned to observe, to assess temporal wrongs from an eternal perspective, to see the temporal world of slavery from an eternal vantage point. *Pain can be a good parent,* teaching us patience and restraint and trust in God.

Peace wasn't valid yet for Joshua. Israel had fallen! Joshua wasn't a prophet who instantly rose to religiously pronounce peace. There was no peace to be had. Some people attempt to deal with trouble by simply smothering it in platitudes, washing the wound in warm, soothing water while hiding the break in the bone! Using phrases that have become insults to the hurting, as we assure them God is in control. But it's us that are in control, though actually out of control, having made a mess! Ai was a mess. It had to be addressed. It had to be corrected!

So, Joshua was in the quiet sanctuary by the Ark of God, leaning on the everlasting arms. In His presence. Waiting upon Him to break this impasse. This wasn't a military problem. Joshua could have fixed that. It was a spiritual problem. He had a few thoughts over this quiet day. In his meditation, a question arose that he couldn't answer. He didn't succumb to pathetic self-blame as a leader. He didn't go into a weepy false repentance. There was a question that he couldn't find an honest answer to… *How could this happen?!* The questions of how and why are important to the believing man of God. Joshua could see as well as any 'what' had happened… have you been there?

Have you suddenly found yourself in a catastrophe? You did everything right, but it all went wrong. Have you been in a church that's been there? You, or the oversight, or the whole congregation, found themselves in a dilemma that they didn't foresee. There was no brainstorming that included the consideration of a failure to their plan. We often call that 'faith'! Of course, discussing the implications of failure, in church projects, can be seen as unbelief. But Joshua had sent spies and discussed numbers and considered these things. The three thousand men were more than enough to defeat Ai. But it was the Lord who was against them.

chapter eighty-six

GOD BEING AGAINST US

Here in this narrative, we are faced with a stark fact that many refuse to consider. The fact is God can be against us. There are things we can do, but there are things God isn't happy about us doing at all, due to failure among us. The solution isn't to admit you can't win them all. Joshua shows us a better way. Go into the quiet place with the Lord. Wait there for a sufficient time... time to hear the voice of God. Then deal with the problem.

And so Joshua said:

Alas, Lord God, why have You brought this people over the Jordan at all—to deliver us into the hand of the Amorites, to destroy us? Oh, that we had been content, and dwelt on the other side of the Jordan! O Lord, what shall I say when Israel turns its back before its enemies? For the Canaanites and all the inhabitants of the land will hear it, and surround us, and cut off our name from the earth. Then what will You do for Your great name?
—Joshua 7:7–9

There is something about this outburst we must recognize. Remember, we are trying to get to know Joshua. Joshua says *why have You...?* Was he blaming God? He said *"...did you bring us over to deliver us...to destroy us?! Our name shall be 'Cut off'"*! And, *"What shall I say...?"* Was he concerned about himself? He then caps this with: *"What are You going to do?"* This was a total disaster in Joshua's mind. But I don't think he was blaming God.

This sounds like a catalogue of complaints against God. No atheist could improve upon it! God is to blame? Our enemy? He's going to destroy us? Joshua asked how he would be able to explain this. Finally, Joshua said: *"What will You do for Your great name?"* Poor Joshua! Even a day of prayerful waiting wasn't enough to ease his troubled mind. What happened? Well, today we would say Joshua was under stress. That's it, 'stress' excuses every aberration. This situation had a cause! Every stressful moment has a cause.

SECTION XVII:
THE PROBLEM IS AMONG OUR OWN 'STUFF'

chapter eighty-seven
GOD NO LONGER WITH US

If we jump ahead, Joshua has just enacted judgement upon Achan. That matter dealt with, the issue is once again Ai, which must be destroyed. In chapter 8 verse 1 the Lord encourages Joshua, don't be "...dismayed." This is an interesting Hebrew word. It means to be "shattered, broken, terrified."[15]

It is frequently used in conjunction with the word 'fear' as in Joshua 8:1: *"Do not be afraid nor be dismayed..."* It would appear from this encouragement that Joshua's response, which we read in chapter 7:7–9, must be understood in the light of him being dismayed! That is, upon seeing the defeat at Ai, Joshua was broken by the news. His confidence in himself and God was shattered. The implications were terrifying for Joshua at every level. His response shouldn't be read as anger or frustration with the situation or with God, even with himself. It was a spiritual breaking. His belief in God's presence was shattered. His passion for the honour of God was broken. This is the level of spirituality that the pastor needs— the concern is God's honour, not our own. This resulted from Joshua's years of learning followed by years of practice.

The Lord was, nevertheless, still angry. The matter must be dealt with. And so, the Lord responds to Joshua strongly. Not to rebuke, but to bring him out of dismay and spur him into action. God's encouraging words come in relation to Ai and its destruction. However, they provide a possible guide to interpreting Joshua's

---

15 W. E. Vine, Merrill Unger, and William White, *Vines Complete Expository Dictionary of Old and New Testament Words* (Thomas Nelson, 1992), 60.

response. Otherwise, he might seem to have completely lost control. The Lord spoke just when Joshua had reached the end of his outburst of ignorance. He still didn't know anything! And so "*the Lord spoke...*" The Lord will always be with us in such confusion. We might have to wait *for* Him, but we must believe *in* Him!

What do you predict when someone says, 'The Lord spoke'? Consider this carefully, because God never changes. He is the same today as in Joshua's day. The same things that angered Him in Joshua's day anger Him today. Today, many churches have forbidden God to be angry with anything! We certainly don't talk about God being angry even in a balanced mix of truth. We aren't comfortable portraying God as angry. We prefer a 'god' who has nothing but love as his total makeup! This is the influence of the world on the church.

A desperate need for acceptance by the world has overtaken churches across the spectrum. The church with the most love is expected to be the winner. But God is more than love. Here, He is still love, but real love can be angry! It's perfectly reasonable to say that God might be angry with what is happening in churches all over the world on Sunday mornings! This doesn't mean He will destroy them... He may pass them by... He tells Joshua if this matter of Achan isn't dealt with "*Neither will I be with you anymore...*"! (Josh 7:12). Soak this up, take it in. Think about what that experience might be like. Feel the depression. Then recognize the text isn't intended to make us think. It is designed to make us act. Some texts are to make us think. Others are to make us act. Often, we get them the wrong way round.

chapter eighty-eight
WORSHIP BEING EXAMINED

The Lord commanded Joshua to *"Get up!"* (Joshua 7:10). Now, this isn't gentle language. This is anger demanding obedience. This language walks over emotions—emotions can be insubstantial, often irrelevant, many times unhelpful, as they are here. Joshua is repentant, and humbly lying on the ground prostrate before the Ark. Yet God unceremoniously reduces Joshua's religious moment to nothing: *"Why do you lie thus on your face…?"* (Josh 7:10). How many times do we have to read such passages and still not learn?

Here we have a genuine moment of religious expression reduced to a matter of divine irritation! Why? Because it isn't relevant. God often accepts worship that is flawed but genuine. But here in Joshua, we see clearly that God expects a certain reality in worship. This isn't the time for humbly repenting of or praying for… 'you know not what.' It isn't the time to remonstrate with God. It is a time for dealing with men, with a man.

There is plenty of evidence that evangelical and reformed churches have lost their way. We are being defeated at every turn! Thinking, rational, and spiritual people, are asking real questions about the state of the church and about the state of the world. Understanding and interest about the Bible has diminished. Churches have no prayer meetings where the whole church attends regularly. A handful of attendees is seen as ok! Perhaps God is asking 'Where is Abel your brother?' (Gen 4:9). And we are not answering.

"Get up! Why do you lie thus on the ground?" (7:10), says a disturbingly powerful voice. While Joshua is questioning God… God is demanding action! Why have we allowed ourselves to be reduced

to empty vessels, broken cisterns, silent witnesses? Why are there so few converts to Christ? Yet no dealing with issues that choke the life out of churches? God will sooner or later come among us and stop the charade. He will startle a church that hasn't addressed its failings. He will bring us to the place where we must deal with sin in our midst, or He will depart. Some may not even notice His absence because we have been performing for ourselves for so long. When we recognize that much of what we do is unreal, maybe unholy, then we too might hear these awful words: *"Get up… Israel has sinned"*! Now… would be pastor, church leader, elder… would you recognize His voice? Perhaps from an unexpected source?

chapter eighty-nine

THE PROBLEM IS AMONG OUR OWN 'STUFF'

Here in Chapter 7:11 we have the Lord telling Joshua the reasons for their failure at Ai. Leadership in God's church is more than the ability to lead. God demands a biblical standard and biblical obedience. Perhaps Joshua is learning here that leaders are still 'servants' of God. This understanding implies both a strength and a humility. It gives leaders the ability to lead and be followed. It makes a man strong in the Lord while lacking confidence in himself. It gives him a high moral standard, which he often fails to obey. He isn't morally superior. The Lord tells Joshua what has happened at Ai and what is required to fix it.

They must go back. We don't like going back. Joshua must go back to the principle of Jericho being 'devoted to destruction.' The devotion offered at Jericho was incomplete. Part of the offering for destruction was stolen. God tells Joshua how to find and complete the devotion of Jericho.

So, Ai wasn't the problem. Jericho was the problem. Jericho was unfinished. Ai shouldn't have been started. Joshua sent men to Ai, but God wasn't with them, so they failed. The problem was entirely internal to the nation of Israel. One Israelite held up the entire campaign. This is a sobering fact, a fundamental principle for churches. Sometimes God isn't interested in the next thing until the last thing is complete.

A church has a time of trouble. Disharmony or worse. Some people leave the church, and with them we suppose the difficulty to be over. They were the cause. However, God wants us to examine ourselves to see how we allowed the trouble to develop and boil to the point of disharmony. Why didn't we see it happen earlier in the year or a decade ago? Were we careless about something? Trouble is seldom the result of one party. We just want to move on and be happy again.

We learn no lessons and accept no responsibility or blame. We reject any notion that we may still have to make peace among ourselves or with the folks who left. Often, we prefer to just let God leave with them! Many church groups haven't missed God since He left. They are still functioning as they did centuries ago without change, proud of their 'consistency.' Their diligent repetition of traditions long since dead.

The Lord tells Joshua what has happened. Someone disobeyed the command of God in Jericho. Specifically, they *"transgressed"* (verse 11). They crossed a boundary. They have also *"taken some of the 'accursed things'"* (verse 12). So, *"They have both stolen and deceived"* (verse 11). They hid them in their tent! So, a very thorough analysis is given by the Lord. He saw it all, every detail. On the human level, thirty-six good men were killed in action as a direct result of Achan's act. More importantly, God's honour was at stake.

Note that the Lord says, *"they have also put it among their own stuff"* (verse 11). The Lord isn't guiding Joshua to Achan here. He is expressing anger that they brought the accursed thing into the camp of Israel! Into their own home and family. Everything was polluted. The fate of Jericho was brought upon themselves. Men are so quick to judge God while being sympathetic to sinners. God gave His Son for us! He is full of love for us, but he is a righteous and holy God and can't look upon sin. Poor Joshua understood all this after years with Moses dealing with Israel in the desert. He understands God's ways, Moses, no doubt, told him. Joshua knew what must happen, but the Lord told him just the same. The sentence has been passed.

Verses 13–19 is the outworking of this until Achan is brought forth. This reflects the judgement of God at the end of time for those who don't believe. We think we can hide, like Achan. But every one of us will be discovered, exposed, and judged. Consider urgently, therefore, that Jesus took that burden upon Himself at Calvary

The Problem Is among Our Own 'Stuff'

and there bore our judgement in His own body on the tree. Joshua understood what God was doing. The Nation of Israel understood too. I expect that today many believers might not! See Joshua's heart expressed when he is presented with Achan...

chapter ninety
BEING GENTLE WITH THE GUILTY

"Now Joshua said to Achan, 'My son, I beg you, give glory to the Lord God of Israel, and make confession to Him, and tell me now what you have done; do not hide it from me'"
—Joshua 7:19

Joshua's approach to Achan is movingly kind. Good men had died. God was turned against His people. Joshua could easily have been angry. Yet His approach is paternal. *"My Son…"* Joshua doesn't demand explanations. He just begs for truth, *"I beg you …"* Joshua's reason for this request is that God may be justified in dealing with His people: *"…give Glory to the Lord God of Israel."* Notice who is important here for Joshua. The confession is to be made to *the Lord God of Israel*. Joshua doesn't adopt a priestly role. He asks for confession to the Lord directly. A confession made directly to the Lord would set things correctly into place.

However, Joshua has a right to know what Achan has done. Joshua requests Achan to tell him. Note Joshua's understanding of the deviousness of the sin: *"Do not hide it from me"*! There is veiled strength here set against Joshua's gentle approach. Achan is being warned on the human level here. Joshua won't allow this moment to spoil Israel.

So that is the way Joshua deals with this situation. He is gentle with the sinner, making it easy, guiding him to the correct hierarchy of responsibility and offence. Joshua helps Achan to understand what he has done before he even confesses. He ends his brief request with a final veiled warning. He says, *"Do not hide it from me"* Implying gently… 'if you aren't afraid of God, be afraid of me.'

Did Joshua's approach work? Yes, it did. So perhaps we should take note of his procedure before we judge someone, guilty or innocent. Only God knows for certain what has happened before there's a confession. And the New Testament reminds us strongly: *"…let him that thinks he stands take heed lest he fall"* (1 Cor. 10:12). Achan confesses to the Lord before Joshua.

chapter ninety-one

THE VALLEY OF TROUBLE

And Achan answered Joshua and said, "Indeed I have sinned against the Lord God of Israel, and this is what I have done: when I saw among the spoils a beautiful Babylonian garment, two hundred shekels of silver, and a wedge of gold weighing fifty shekels, I coveted them and took them. And there they are, hidden in the earth in the midst of my tent, with the silver under it."

—Joshua 7:20, 21

How often we confess sin, and if we were to listen to ourselves, we would stop and start again! Often, we are full of justification, prevarications, qualifications. Achan seems to recognize the truth about himself. "*I have sinned... against the Lord... This is what I have done... And there it is in my tent.*" Yet, however thorough his confession, it didn't reduce the seriousness of the sin. It doesn't reduce the necessity to put things back in order. What a humbling thing for any sinner, to have to enact punishment on another sinner. Joshua can have no such luxury as to consider his own humanity at this moment. He is Israel's leader and God's representative, and he must follow through. Joshua must enact judgement and punishment.

Achan is taken, and all his family, his goods, and all he had stolen (Joshua 7:24–26). They stone them to death and then the stolen goods from Jericho are devoted to destruction as they should have been at Jericho. The Lord turned from the fierceness of His anger.

As I write on these biblical moments, I am aware of an interesting human response that arises to God's judgements. We object! Vocal or silent, there is a resistance to judgement within the human heart. There would be no need for judgement if we would obey. It is us who sin not God. And judgement is what we are reminded of in these verses. There is a judgement coming, and all who have trusted in Jesus Christ will be spared—because Jesus has already born the punishment for our sins.

When metal has been worked on, it is often heated then left to cool naturally. This used to be called 'normalizing.' It allowed the tensions and stress in the metal to relax. Tensions make metal (and people) prone to distortion and breaking. Justice enacted properly brings satisfaction. Satisfaction is experiential knowledge, the sense that everything has been 'normalized.' In Israel, there was peace in the air.

This took place in the Valley of Achor, the valley of 'trouble.' Isaiah says when God's people seek Him, He will make this same valley, "...*a place for herds to lie down*" (Isaiah 65:10). Hosea speaks similarly saying, The Lord will "... *give her... the valley of Achor as a door of hope; she shall sing there, as in the days of her youth, as in the days when she came up from the land of Egypt*" (Hosea 2:15). What a glorious transformation of a name?!

Have you known this "Valley of Achor"? Has trouble dragged you down? Put your trust in Him. He can turn life around. When we hear His voice and obey, trouble is replaced with, "... *joy inexpressible and full of glory*" (1 Peter 1:8). Only faith in God can take the worst of places and transforms them into the best. This is our God!

SECTION XVIII:
BEING BACK TO WHERE YOU STARTED

chapter ninety-two
GOD IS GENTLE WITH JOSHUA

Joshua 8:1–13

"Now the Lord said to Joshua: 'Do not be afraid, nor be dismayed…'"
—Joshua 8:1

This sounds like Joshua chapter one! The Lord must remind Joshua not to be afraid or dismayed. Clearly, the situation at Ai dealt him a blow. He had taken Jericho, but then in his own eyes, at Ai, he had failed. He had done no wrong, but he knew there was something wrong. There were consequences. It was early in the campaign. The Lord encouraged him not to be afraid or dismayed. Always understand that God sees us as we are, not as others see us. God knows us. He wants us to truly know ourselves. To be who we really are. Too many people live fantasy lives, creating personas based on other people. We are individuals.

Jesus talks about two men going up to the Temple to pray. The tax collector and the Pharisee.

The tax collector sums us up. We are sinful; this knowledge keeps us humble. This humble tax collector knew that the essential aspect of his character was his sinfulness. The Pharisee tells the truth about himself. He isn't like other men, and he does the things he says. But he is totally ignorant about what God sees: his pride and arrogance.

A real warning for pastors is to note that even in the presence of God, in His house, we can act, being a lie! We may stand out from the crowd outside of God's temple, but before Him, we are all the same. Among men, we may stand head and shoulders above others. Our reality is only seen in the presence of God. Joshua knew he was just like other men when he stood before God. Joshua was like the tax collector; he understood his sinful nature. For this reason, the lord tells him not to be afraid.

Dismay is a constant danger to the man who knows his own sinfulness. Some men hide behind their one moment of holiness. Other men are disabled with their one sin. God doesn't want us to trust in our successes nor be dismayed by our failures. He wants us to trust Him alone. The Lord warmly calls Joshua, and us, to walk in His strength. So, the Lord tells Joshua to get up and go to Ai. Service for God, like praise, should be uplifting. The Lord gave Joshua instructions. Joshua is back in the harness… being obedient. *"The Lord is a man of war…"* (Exod. 15:3). Joshua 8:1–13 tells us the battle plan and the tactics to set in place. Verse 2 is an assurance of success.

chapter ninety-three
DOING THINGS RIGHT

Joshua 8: 9–13

The strategy laid out previously worked. We are given the details of the plan and the battle. In the previous campaign, Joshua said, "... *Do not weary all the people there, for the people of Ai are few*" (Joshua 7:3). This time he hears the Lord speak: "... *take all the people of war...*" (Josh. 8:1). He takes thirty thousand men. The city of Ai was taken and destroyed.

The information and details here show that the Lord gives full attention to small things, and we must seek Him, especially when we are confident of our plan. God's ways are not our ways. Joshua's training under Moses and in Egypt came to his aid but only when instructed by the Lord. This is a problem for natural leaders. They think they can do things without God. But they can't. They think they have learned everything needed, but they have not.

chapter ninety-four

JOSHUA RENEWS THE COVENANT

Now Joshua built an altar to the Lord God of Israel in Mount Ebal,. Half of them were in front of Mount Gerizim and half of them in front of Mount Ebal... And afterward he read all the words of the law, the blessings and the curses... There was not a word of all that Moses had commanded which Joshua did not read before all the assembly of Israel, with the women, the little ones, and the strangers who were living among them.
—Joshua 8:30, 33–35

We see that Joshua wasn't only focussed on winning battles and conquering land. He knew when to stop and offer thanksgiving and rededication. He took the nation back to its beginning. He reset them between two great principles, the blessings and the curses of God's law. Joshua showed an incredible balance. He was a great warrior; he was becoming a great statesman. He was a believer first, in everything.

How unbalanced we have become in our preaching. The people have no stomach for a sermon on obedience. A life of obedience can appear cold. Love and holiness seem contradictory to us. We choose to love exclusively, yet Jesus said: *"If you love Me, keep My commandments..."* (John 14:15). But here at these two mountains, with half of the people on Ebal and the other half on Gerizim, Joshua reminded them not just of holiness but also of "curses." What are we to make of this?

Sin is what brings down the curses spoken of in this narrative. God forbid that this book should detract from the fullness of the work of Christ on the cross. But God help us if we simply ignore what the very existence of these same curses tells us. *'The'* curse was laid upon Him who bore it for us. But sin in its very nature is cursed. There is an element of natural flow in the spiritual life, in the moral life, even in the physical life. This flow is between blessing and cursing in many expressions. The curses are there to warn the careless, the rebellious. There are serious warnings with consequences. These consequences are not always a direct act of God. They are more often the direct result of sinful acts. Of course, God is angry with the wicked every day. He deals with them justly, and His judgements are measured.

Balanced preaching references both sides of this pendulum. Read God's Word, walk with God, obey God's Word, live for Christ and your neighbour. Curses are for those who refuse to do these things. But we all fail. Preaching the law and its curses awakens the conscience and causes men to run to Christ for mercy... and find it! In our deliberations on this area, we should remember Romans 8: *"There is therefore now no condemnation to those who are in Christ Jesus, who do not walk according to the flesh, but according to the Spirit"* (Romans 8:1). This text is saying that those who are truly in Christ walk in the Spirit.

Finally, on this topic, too large for this book, we need to revise our understanding of "blessing." We have reduced the subject to mere happiness or good health. Neither of these is necessarily a blessing. His presence here and now is the greatest of this life's blessings. Spiritual blessings are independent of the material or the physical. The blessing of being 'in Christ' removes all fear of the curse of the law.

> *And it came to pass when all the kings who were on this side of the Jordan, in the hills and in the lowland and in all the coasts of the Great Sea toward Lebanon—the Hittite, the Amorite, the Canaanite, the Perizzite, the Hivite, and*

the Jebusite—heard about it, that they gathered together to fight with Joshua and Israel with one accord.
—Joshua 9:1–2

Israel's victories garnish a much larger foe. Their victory over little Ai raised the wrath of a larger foe. *Being Joshua* is intended to illustrate the spiritual fight of the believer's daily life. The fight with sin inside and out, with evil inside and out. Christian warfare is never about guns or physical violence. Freedom of speech allows for strong language when it is required. It is required today from the church to illustrate God's anger at wickedness and thereby to restrain wickedness, for the glory of God and the good of our grandchildren. It is painfully lacking. Many old sermons by great, renowned men wouldn't be acceptable in today's church. But then neither are some of the Old Testament prophets!

Christians today often want peace on earth. This is often a desire for heaven brought down to earth. Joshua understood that life was a battle. People get hurt in battles, but victory brings a better world. The premise of this book is that the church isn't fighting the good fight of faith. Some have substituted fighting ethical and social battles for the fight of faith. They aren't the same. The world fights for social and ethical standards. The work we aren't engaging in is witness to the truth of God and evangelism on the personal level. Of course, some are.

Joshua also understood that peace is only real after problems have been dealt with. He knew that Canaan was a battlefield until it was subdued. Canaan is a partial picture of heaven; but now, for Israel, Canaan was all about fighting.

The response of the world is seldom capitulation. They gathered to deal with Israel. Few things produce unity like adversity. However, the narrative doesn't take us straight to this threat. An interlude breaks in upon the narrative. People aren't always what they seem. Another essential to learn for any leader of God's church. The Gibeonites bring 'craft' into the 'art of war.'

SECTION XIX:
BEING DECEIVED

chapter ninety-five
THE DECEPTION OF GIBEON

Joshua 9:3–15. The essential text for our discussion is verses 14–15:

Then the men of Israel took some of their provisions; but they did not ask counsel of the Lord. So Joshua made peace with them, and made a covenant with them to let them live; and the rulers of the congregation swore to them.
—Joshua 9:14–15

Here we have the root of the problem. They decided and acted "*...but they did not ask counsel of the Lord*" (verse 14). Joshua began a conversation with the Gibeonites before He had a conversation with God. This is a common problem in churches and individual believers today. We love dialogue. Do not be as secure in your thoughts as Joshua was. Most of the time we only consult the Lord when we don't know what to do. Joshua acted on his own understanding. He forgot that every situation requires God's input. As early as the Garden of Eden, a question for the attentive reader is: 'Why did Eve get into a conversation with the serpent?' Where was Adam? Well, Joshua got into a conversation with the Gibeonites, and that was all it took for the Gibeonite deception to be cemented.

Some might say it was because Joshua was tired after Jericho and Ai! Perhaps, but this just ratifies the point. He should have known himself well enough to know if he was tired. However, the reason we should always engage the Lord isn't simply because we are weak. It is to acknowledge that He is needed and involved in all aspects of our lives. He is outworking a plan we shall see fully in eternity.

So, after the briefest of conversations, Joshua covenants with complete strangers. A binding covenant! Not even a week passes before it all backfires.

Pastors beware of tiredness. Church workers beware of overwork. Believers stay healthy and in control of your whole being. Do what is necessary. Set it as a daily norm to look after yourself. Love your neighbour "... as yourself." Days off are just modern business practices invading the church. Real pastoral work may not allow for a day off this week but may allow for the whole of next week off, and the same in reverse. In a normal week, a day off may or may not be required. The wisest standard for dedicated pastors is take 'sufficient' time off. Only you know what the detail of that is. Decide before God. Make sure your congregation understand that you are not lazy. You should be able to work for as many days as it takes to handle a matter. But in general, look after yourself or you will become unable to help anyone. Joshua should have known himself by now. He made a mistake. He did not take counsel from the Lord.

Joshua 9:16–23

Too often in the affairs of men, the decisions of the rulers adversely affect the people. The people they are supposed to protect are hurt by failed governance. In the modern Western world, these people declare themselves proudly as 'servants' of the people. But they seem too easily to lose this understanding and 'lord it' over the people. We see this in every democracy from time to time. The form of church government that prevails in a church often determines the treatment of the congregation. What an error, to declare the oversight of a church as "managers"! The same mentality replaced the Bible with a constitution, I expect!

However, Joshua isn't really a servant of the people; he is absolutely their leader. Joshua is the God-appointed leader of Israel. Israel was a theocracy. God was its ultimate king. Joshua was His representative. Joshua and the Lord were a team. And Joshua shut Him out of this matter; the people were hurt and justifiably angry.

The rulers, when confronted by the people, fell back on a principle. "... *We have sworn to them by the Lord God of Israel; now therefore, we may not touch them*" (verse 19). This is a powerful argument. It carries an air of high standards. Joshua goes on to implicate God: "*...lest wrath be upon us because of the oath which we swore to them*" (verse 20). He infers that God will punish them for failure to keep an oath. One can't help but think their original 'oath,' to guide God's children and protect them, superseded any future oath. Joshua swore to lead the people of God and failed to do so resulting in a problem. Shouldn't he have fulfilled the first oath rather than the second? God told Joshua to do something; Joshua told the Gibeonites he would do something else. He is effectively ignoring what God told him in favour of keeping his word, and Joshua does this citing God's commands as his reason! This kind of rationale is common in churches today.

> *Then Joshua called for them, and he spoke to them, saying, "Why have you deceived us, saying, 'We are very far from you,' when you dwell near us? Now therefore, you are cursed, and none of you shall be freed from being slaves—woodcutters and water carriers for the house of my God."*
> —Joshua 9:22–23

chapter ninety-six

LEADERS BEING FOOLED

Joshua 9:24–27

The Gibeonites seem to have heard and understood the command Joshua said he would fulfill. They quote it: "... *the Lord your God commanded His servant Moses to give you all the land, and to destroy all the inhabitants of the land...*" (Joshua 9:24).

We can be guilty of lessoning God's judgement to ease our own discomfort. Avoid this and enact God's ways—we become spiritually mature when we commit to doing what God tells us, not just abstaining from what he has forbidden. Sometimes we feel that restrictions (don't do that) are harder than actions (do this). Both, in their context and correctly understood, tend to be counter to our human state. Both require active obedience regardless of the cost.

Calvin in his commentary on Joshua says:

> blame is justly due to the foolish credulity of Joshua and the rulers... Yet the Lord who is wont to bring light out of darkness, turned it to the advantage of His people... So we should see in this situation God turning Joshua's failing to Israel's advantage. The Kings were gathering. Gibeon was a large nation and their pact with Israel weakened and upset the other nations of Canaan.[16]

---

16 Calvin's Commentary Volume IV, Joshua Psalms (Grand Rapids, Michigan: Baker Book House), 137ff.

Now it came to pass when Adoni-Zedek king of Jerusalem heard how Joshua had taken Ai and had utterly destroyed it—as he had done to Jericho and its king, so he had done to Ai and its king—and how the inhabitants of Gibeon had made peace with Israel and were among them, that they feared greatly, because Gibeon was a great city, like one of the royal cities, and because it was greater than Ai, and all its men were mighty. Therefore Adoni-Zedek king of Jerusalem sent to Hoham king of Hebron, Piram king of Jarmuth, Japhia king of Lachish, and Debir king of Eglon, saying, "Come up to me and help me, that we may attack Gibeon, for it has made peace with Joshua and with the children of Israel."

—Joshua 10:1–4

In these verses, we are told that Gibeon was a "*Great City,*" a "*Royal City.*" We can understand this caused upset among the other nations of Canaan. This is where we find ourselves in chapter 10 of Joshua.

Verse 4 introduces some amazing events. We will see that the world often unites against those who make a pact with, or "... made peace with Israel." For my entire life, reading the daily news about the state of Israel has been like reading the historical biblical records.

"*Come up to me and help me, that we may attack Gibeon, for it has made peace with Joshua and with the children of Israel*" (Joshua 10: 4).

A world united against God's people is initially frightening. Who wouldn't fear? This book isn't about the attacks on Christianity today, but it is happening. This book is about how God prepares believers, making them strong men and women of God who can stand against this onslaught and prevail. It isn't a college diploma course or an apologetics course. This preparation is constant and lifelong. We are looking at Joshua. Here we find lessons of how he became able to take Israel into the Promised Land and overcome evil. The lessons Joshua learned are the lessons every believer needs to understand and experience. Joshua has a new battle to fight, but what God spoke to him earlier is still fundamentally relevant.

chapter ninety-seven

FAITH IS INSTANT

And the men of Gibeon sent to Joshua at the camp at Gilgal, saying, "Do not forsake your servants; come up to us quickly, save us and help us, for all the kings of the Amorites who dwell in the mountains have gathered together against us."

So Joshua ascended from Gilgal, he and all the people of war with him, and all the mighty men of valor. And the Lord said to Joshua, "Do not fear them, for I have delivered them into your hand; not a man of them shall stand before you." Joshua therefore came upon them suddenly, having marched all night from Gilgal.

—Joshua 10:6-9

Remember the first instruction God gave to Joshua: *"Be strong and of good courage; do not be afraid..."* (Joshua 1: 9). This is an exhortation in the form of a command. Joshua's response to the plea for help from Gibeon demonstrates this control of fear, this courage in the face of attack. He rises and travels all night to deal with the threat facing those who just recently were on the same side as these five kings.

The rejection of fear and the exercise of faith that produced courage was generated in chapter one by the word of God to Joshua. God's commands aren't merely external. When we grasp His commands by faith, we receive the necessary energy to fulfill them. The practical action required to confront the circumstances is already there when God's Word is internalized by faith.

The challenge isn't the battle, the challenge is believing God is with us. Could this be why the name given to describe the incarnate deity is Immanuel, 'God with us'! The belief and trust in God's Word produce all the believer needs to live for God in an alien world.

Joshua's challenge was met long before the five kings came against Gibeon. Hence the instant nature of his response. He required no time or hype. When faith is active as a daily norm, we can march all night and fight all day against all odds and win. Israel, Jesus's 'little flock' (Luke 12:32), is more powerful than all the might of Canaan's warrior kings.

chapter ninety-eight

LEADERS MUST BE THOROUGH

Joshua routes the five kings:

So the Lord routed them before Israel, killed them with a great slaughter at Gibeon, chased them along the road that goes to Beth Horon, and struck them down as far as Azekah and Makkedah. And it happened, as they fled before Israel and were on the descent of Beth Horon, that the Lord cast down large hailstones from heaven on them as far as Azekah, and they died.

—Joshua 10:10–12

See God's identification with Joshua in this part of the story—Joshua had responded in faith. The Lord saw his fearless stand against the world, came to his aid, and engaged the enemy on his behalf. Never doubt when you have stood for God and His Word and the battle rages that God is with you. He is always attending His children, individually, at the same time, without a ripple of stress. Joshua's battle wasn't finished. Joshua understood that God finishes what He starts. Although Joshua was fighting against five heathen kings, he knew victory was assured: God will deliver Israel. The Lord will finish the battle.

Then Joshua spoke to the Lord in the day when the Lord delivered up the Amorites before the children of Israel, and he said in the sight of Israel: "Sun, stand still over Gibeon; And Moon, in the Valley of Aijalon." ... Is this not written in the Book of Jasher? ... So the sun stood still... And there has been no day like that, before it or after it, that the Lord heeded the voice of a man; for the Lord fought for Israel.

—Joshua 10:12–14

   This is a remarkable moment in the Bible. When we first read this text, we are inclined to think there has been a mistake in the translation. Surely it was God, not Joshua, that spoke to the Sun and the Moon to stand still?! Well, the Bible seems to anticipate that we might doubt such a remarkable event and verifies that it was Joshua. In the above text, it references *"the book of Jasher"* (a document lost to us but with evidence that it existed) and that *"...there had been no day like that, before it..."* It then goes on with an air of prophetic certainty to say *"...nor after it..."* Some things can't be repeated. The Lord sent great hailstones and let Joshua stop the sun and the moon for a day to finish what He started. Five against one is a bit unfair. Bullies always get their due sooner or later. Here it was little Israel and the Lord of Hosts that defeated these five kings. We too can expect the Lord to help us in private and corporate battles as His church.

chapter ninety-nine
THE BATTLE IS NOT THE END OF THE EVENT

Joshua 10:16–27

"*But these five kings had fled and hidden themselves in a cave at Makkedah*" (Joshua 10:16). The name "Makkedah" means "a place of shepherds."[17]

A place of shepherds, what a beautiful name! We can easily imagine shepherds bedding down there for the night, carrying a sick lamb, watching for wolves, transforming that cold, dark cave with pastoral warmth. When Joshua gets there, it's filled with terror. The hallowed resting place was desecrated by the warrior kings' cowering. Never forget that soldiers die; we honour them, but often their leaders live. These kings fled and hid in this place of shepherds.

See the stark contrast with Jesus, our king. He went to the battle on the cross alone, fought the fight alone, tore the gates of hell asunder alone. They put Him in a dark cave… alone. He filled it with resurrection light and power. He rolled the stone away and rose triumphant over death and hell… our enemies defeated. Now He leads His flock beside still waters, He restores their souls, and we will dwell with Him forever.

And it was told Joshua, saying, "The five kings have been found hidden in the cave at Makkedah" (Joshua 10:17). Perhaps it was the very shepherds whose evening comfort was spoiled that reported their whereabouts.

---

17 Merrill Tenney, Zondervan's Bible Dictionary (Grand Rapids, Michigan: Zondervan, 1967), 503.

> *Then Joshua said, "Open the mouth of the cave, and bring out those five kings to me from the cave." And they did so, and brought out those five kings to him from the cave: the king of Jerusalem, the king of Hebron, the king of Jarmuth, the king of Lachish, and the king of Eglon.*
> —Joshua 10:22–23

Think about these five kings. They were infamous. They lived lives worthy of God's judgements. They were warned by the Exodus. They were warned while Israel was in the desert. They were warned by the devotion of Jericho to destruction. Yet even their terror produced no repentance and didn't call upon God. God saw that there was only hardness of heart, hatred against God and His people. They wanted death, and God gave them their hearts' desire—Joshua enacted God's wrath upon His enemies.

Joshua's captains, ordinary men, against five kings. The captains were ordinary men. At heart, they wanted to build homes and raise children, become farmers and shepherds.

God wants to take ordinary believers and empower them to do great feats of bravery. God will put us into situations designed to bring us to maturity in His service. We can become what we need to be, having been trained in past events.

It appears that these powerful kings still brought some fear into the hearts of Israel. Joshua wanted to remove all fear of God's enemies from them. He orchestrated their final defeat.

> *So it was, when they brought out those kings to Joshua, that Joshua called for all the men of Israel, and said to the captains of the men of war who went with him, "Come near, put your feet on the necks of these kings." And they drew near and put their feet on their necks. Then Joshua said to them, "Do not be afraid, nor be dismayed; be strong and of good courage, for thus the Lord will do to all your enemies against whom you fight."*
> —Joshua 10:24–25

The Battle is Not the End of the Event

Note that the word spoken by the Lord to Joshua became the word spoken by Joshua to his captains. The man of God must remember God's dealings and translate them to those under his care.

> *And afterward Joshua struck them and killed them, and hanged them on five trees; and they were hanging on the trees until evening... Joshua commanded, and they took them down from the trees, cast them into the cave where they had been hidden, and laid large stones against the cave's mouth, which remain until this very day.*
> —Joshua 10: 26–27

Joshua brought his captains to the kings... to put their feet on their necks. This finalized the moment and showed them that kings are just men, just the same as any other man. Joshua also showed them that God is God.

SECTION XX:
PROMISE BEING FULFILLED

chapter one hundred
OF THE SOUTHLAND

Joshua 10:28–43

For the purpose of this book, Joshua 10: 28–43 can be summarized by quoting verse 40. The historical record says: *"So Joshua conquered all the land: the mountain country and the South and the lowland and the wilderness slopes, and all their kings; he left none remaining, but utterly destroyed all that breathed, as the Lord God of Israel had commanded."* This isn't a statement about Joshua though his name is attached for the record. This is a statement of the many promises made by God to His servant Abraham being fulfilled.

Joshua returned to Gilgal when this part of the campaign reached a break. Gilgal, meaning "circle of stones," was the first place Israel camped after crossing the Jordan. Here, Joshua restored the rite of circumcision in response to God's promise to: "Role away the reproach of Egypt. According to Josephus, Gilgal was about ten miles from the Jordan and two miles or more from Jericho."[18]

This camp represented much for Joshua. Getting Israel over the Jordan and camped at Gilgal was his first real achievement as Moses's successor. Now, he has lots of achievements to reflect upon. He had conquered a great part of Canaan, and he would continue to conquer. However, problems arise of a whole different character, many within Israel itself, which will test Joshua. Battles within

---

18 Merrill Tenney, Zondervan's Bible Dictionary (Grand Rapids, Michigan: Zondervan, 1967), 314.

the church are much harder to take than war with the world. These represent lessons for the church to observe and learn from. Even the redeemed are prone to trouble.

chapter one hundred and one

THE NORTHERN CONQUEST

Joshua 11:1–7

The story thus far has been about the conquest of the southern kingdoms of Canaan. Now an account is given of the northern conquest.

> *And it came to pass, when Jabin king of Hazor heard these things, that he sent to Jobab king of Madon, to the king of Shimron, to the king of Achshaph, and to the kings who were from the north, in the mountains, in the plain south of Chinneroth, in the lowland, and in the heights of Dor on the west, to the Canaanites in the east and in the west, the Amorite, the Hittite, the Perizzite, the Jebusite in the mountains, and the Hivite below Hermon in the land of Mizpah. So they went out, they and all their armies with them, as many people as the sand that is on the seashore in multitude, with very many horses and chariots. And when all these kings had met together, they came and camped together at the waters of Merom to fight against Israel.*
> —Joshua 11:1–5

Until now, Joshua's largest battle was with five kings. These new foes are listed by which part of the country they came from. Then they are simply described as "*...the sand that is on the seashore in multitude, with very many horses and chariots*" (verse 4). Life can be like this. The last problem can appear like nothing compared to the next one. The next often comes too soon. Our responses to such trials can make or break us. For the believer, it is an opportunity to trust God, an invitation to rest in Him by faith. It can even be a command to stand still and see the salvation of God. Even a familiar problem requires faith and a listening ear. Every problem calls us to stand up and be strong. Often, under these extremes, the Lord speaks to encourage us as He does here for Joshua:

"But the Lord said to Joshua, 'Do not be afraid because of them, for tomorrow about this time I will deliver all of them slain before Israel. You shall hamstring their horses and burn their chariots with fire'" (Joshua 11:6).

This verse illustrates how engaged the Lord was with Joshua and Israel. He already knows what He will do, and He tells Joshua. God will deal with this multitude—in twenty-four hours or less! Joshua was listening. Are we? This is our God. Never assume that the problem will linger forever. The Lord can deal with it in a day!

"So Joshua and all the people of war with him came against them suddenly by the waters of Merom, and they attacked them" (Joshua 11:7). This one word sums up the battle strategy and its success: *"Suddenly."* How many of life's battles are lost or won by timing? How many people have fallen by a sudden temptation, a sudden insult, a sudden tragedy? Something unforeseen? Joshua was always ready. He planned to attack them suddenly. Meanwhile, the enemy was resting at the quiet waters of Merom. They weren't ready to fight. Joshua was! Are you ready to do what the Lord asks you, simple or grand?

chapter one hundred and two
TIMING

Joshua set out to attack as soon as he knew they were at Merom. Joshua's enemies assumed they would attack Joshua and win. They assumed he would be afraid, hence their lazy day at Merom. They were wrong. Israel attacked suddenly. Joshua knew how to deal with fear, take instant action, and what action to take.

Timing is important in many areas. Many temptations aren't strong in themselves. They can easily be spurned if you deal with them promptly.

Again, timing is important when listening to preaching. Teaching is for the long-term. Preaching is a moment! The sermon must be understood as a conversation, not an education. I am talking about the main purpose of the sermon. It's for right now. God wants a response right now. Your notes may be useless on Wednesday. Experience the moment. Listen. A myriad of human needs are met as the sermon is delivered. Often sermons are like manna, they last a day then they are superseded.

chapter one hundred and three
LEAVE NOTHING UNDONE

Joshua 11:8–15

For the purpose of this book, verse 15 is a summary of this section.

"As the Lord had commanded Moses His servant, so Moses commanded Joshua, and so Joshua did. He left nothing undone of all that the Lord had commanded Moses."

Here is a worthy goal for our lives: *"He left nothing undone of all that the Lord had commanded..."* Many of us live without any sense that God has commanded anything! Yet He has! Many commands are present in the New Testament. Although we are under grace, there are commands to be obeyed, threaded throughout the New Testament like gold embroidery. Joshua understood that his life was best lived when given away to God and to people.

Joshua 11:16—Summary of Joshua's Conquests

"Thus Joshua took all this land..." This is awesome. What is also amazing is that none of the nations of Canaan made peace with Israel. Sometimes in life, people may refuse to be at peace with us. They appear to take pleasure in making life difficult. Try as we might, peace isn't always possible. We must deal with these people strongly, not enable or sanction their murmuring or complaining. The Bible has laid out procedures for such difficulties. The third amazing thing is that few churches enact these procedures—they avoid them.

chapter one hundred and four
BEING GENEROUS

"So Joshua took the whole land, according to all that the Lord had said to Moses; and Joshua gave it as an inheritance to Israel according to their divisions by their tribes. Then the land rested from war"
—Joshua 11:23

What Joshua took, he gave away. Interesting thought. Surely the Lord gives us whatever we have to be given to His people, His church. This magnanimous spirit is godlike—He gave His only begotten Son for us. Jesus, as quoted by the Apostle Paul, said, *"It is more blessed to give than to receive"* (Acts 20:35). Giving isn't seen as being better than receiving in the world today. Joshua was an example of godliness in his giving. This is the kind of lesson God teaches us in preparing us to serve His church.

Wealth is a sign of success in the world. God gives different evidence of success. His blessing is what we seek. And yet we don't actually 'seek' anything for ourselves. We seek His glory not our own. Whether He sends wealth or poverty, we praise Him contentedly. The 'beatitudes' (Matt 5:1-12) are a set of radical blessings. Find them in Mathew 5:1–12. Be amazed at the words Jesus spoke. Consider them if you would be His child, and if you want to serve Him—remember them! Beautiful attitudes are worth more than gold.

Now the story turns to a historical record of Joshua's accomplishments. This isn't written to boast about Joshua or Israel. It is written to glorify God and to provide historical records. God knew that in the future men would refuse to believe that Israel achieved such success. So here it is recorded for us to see. These records have been consistently and mercilessly examined yet found to be true. There aren't as many critics today as there were fifty years ago.

In New Testament times and today, the church reads these records in spiritual terms. We aren't fighting for land—we have a promised home in heaven, and we are ambassadors for Christ. We want to convince the world that God is our maker, our judge, and our saviour—to be the salt of the earth and bring people to Christ. That is our 'fight.'

This word "fight" needs a review. It doesn't just mean armed conflict, and it isn't necessarily bad. It can be very good indeed! A doctor fights to save someone's life. What about fighting to stay fit? Christian warfare requires restraint more often than attack. It requires silence more often than shouting. It calls for loving your enemies not hating anyone! It also requires the ability to expose evil and present a clear reason for the way people are.

chapter one hundred and five
SIX YEARS OF PROBLEMS INTO ONE SHORT SENTENCE

Joshua 12:1-24

This passage is another summary of Joshua's conquests. Note that this impressive list represents six years of warfare. The Bible compresses six years into two paragraphs. These six years weren't ordinary, they were filled with struggle, fear, and hard work to conquer new land. However, they do represent a certain norm—men fighting, winning, or losing—a universal theme since the fall in the Garden.

There have been wars on every continent and in every century till this very day. Joshua fought evil nations and removed a scourge from the land of Canaan. Israel had been slaves for four hundred years. No other nation tried to free them. Nobody came to their aid. God freed them and promised them a land of their own. He promised Abraham the land of Canaan, and He raised Moses to deliver them from Egypt. They were alone in the world, yet God defeated their enemies, purged Canaan of evil, and settled His people there. It was (and is) their Promised Land.

A note on dealing with difficulty and trouble. Think about your difficulties and observe how long you can talk about your latest hospital result. Listen to the church today whining and whimpering over their difficulties. Note that these are seldom related to their identity as believers. They reflect unbelievers just as well! Yet somebody has told the Christian church that heaven has already begun. We have given converts an expectation of ease via the gospel. The Bible gives no such assurance. It requires plainly that we take up a cross… daily.

Would be pastor, will you be an example of cross-bearing? Or will you choose the congregation that pays the highest stipend? If you think like that, please stay away from pastoral work. You won't be happy until you learn to rejoice in tribulation.

Now, just a brief note to address any critics of Joshua. Many great leaders couldn't restrain themselves with one land. They conquered continents simply because they could! Often needlessly, always cruelly. The 'Roman Peace' came at a price. Joshua fought for one land. Having conquered it, he didn't carry on. He stopped. And… they are still living there all these centuries later. Joshua defeated the armies of Canaan, cleaned the land, shut Jericho up, and closed Jericho down. Then he retired.

Joshua's eighty-six years of hardship is reduced here to just a few sentences. God can transform your years of trouble, even a lifetime of trouble, to a summary sentence. You may still have memories, but God can so transform your life that past pains trouble you no more. They become no more than a summary sentence. Don't hold on to pain God has removed. Don't carry your pains or your doubts into the pulpit or the youth group.

By faith, you can come to the place where you are even able to laugh and tell how God helped you in life's battles. You might not remember them at all… can you imagine that? God can so bless you that past pain can be forgotten. Joshua's victories over trouble have become our inspiration. We can inspire others, in that we no longer need to talk about our troubles. In this narrative, Joshua isn't dead yet. He still has a life to lead. The last battle is death itself, and Joshua isn't dead yet.

chapter one hundred and six
PREPARE FOR OLD AGE

Joshua 13:1–7

"Now Joshua was old, advanced in years. And the Lord said to him: 'You are old, advanced in years, and there remains very much land yet to be possessed'"
—Joshua 13:1

Joshua is old, and the work wasn't complete. An amazing amount had been accomplished in six years, but *"there remains very much land yet to be possessed."* Many old men refuse to come to terms with age and its 'friends.' They feel much younger than their age but only in some ways. The truth is we grow old. Others welcome old age long before it comes. They retire and stop fighting life and its difficulties. There aren't easy answers to these dangers, but a word from God can energize those who have sat down too quickly. Joshua's time to rest was approaching. God tells him straight, *"You are old, advanced in years..."*!

God speaks to lift us and enable us to live a real life, not a fake life. We need to know who we are, what our circumstances are, and what needs to be done. Pleasantries are neither here nor there. When God speaks, His voice lifts the spirit. Joshua had observed this since before Moses died. The Lord told Joshua what remained to be done. As you read the list in verses 2–6 of all that work, you will feel as exhausted as dear Joshua must have felt.

Now, it is hard to imagine Joshua feeling tired. He was a fighter, but the truth must have been reflected in his age, or the Lord wouldn't have declared it. Generally, when God speaks to the faithful soul, they recognize the truth of what is being said. They have thought about it before the Lord spoke. The Lord encouraged him. He says, "... *them I will drive out from before the children of Israel*" (Joshua 13:6) Joshua may have felt an unusual relief. But notice his work, his service, didn't have to end simply because he was too old to fight battles anymore. The Lord gave him a fresh challenge at around ninety years of age! Joshua became a statesman overnight. But his whole life had taught him about land, geography, people, tribes, and nations. Here's his new job: "...*only divide it by lot to Israel as an inheritance, as I have commanded you...*" (verse 6). He is blessed to be given the charge of separating the land to the tribes and giving them their inheritance. What a blessing for a man of war. No longer!

chapter one hundred and seven
BORDERS ARE ESSENTIAL

Joshua 14:15b says, *"Then the land had rest from war."* The war referred to was the recent six years. Their rest would be disturbed again with troubles that weren't wars as such, but they would have wars and rumours of wars until the end of time. Indeed, to this day, there are enemies of Israel who have publicly sworn to annihilate them. But for now, the language of war will be superseded by what follows in Joshua 15:1–12.

The word "border" is mentioned around twenty times in these verses. These borders separated the tribes. The tribes were separated by rivers, valleys, mountains, and seas. The ascent up a hill, a mere brook, can stop one land from another. Little things and big things all contribute to this sense of division. The idea is that almost anything can be used as a border between us as God's people. But these are good! Distinction isn't bad! It has always been understood as a safety mechanism that kept people from one another in a healthy, orderly society. Today we call it "racist." That is an evil word but an ignorant comment.

Here, the word of God sets boundaries between families, extending to tribes, and the nation has a set boundary. Borders give a healthy sense of belonging and ownership, rights, and responsibilities. Be careful who owns the land you decide to go to, to find whatever it is you are looking for. Joshua had seen it all. He was a slave without borders. Everyone could walk all over him. Nothing was marked out as his. He escaped from that unbearable situation, only to find himself a wanderer in a desert. Though it had few borders, he treated these with respect. Now he had a land, and Joshua created borders.

Being Joshua

Our bodies are covered by a border of skin. We have terrible words to describe the invasion of it. There are rules, laws, and penalties including death for invading this border. It is well defined. We are physical entities with boundaries, to be fought for if invaded. If someone gets too close, not even touching, we shy away. To merely touch this border uninvited is abuse.

You can be my neighbour and visit, you may stay for vacations, but we have the right to remove you! Even if you are family but refuse to keep the rules, we can remove you. Human beings are friendly in general but naturally protective of boundaries. No borders… is a war waiting to happen.

Be careful about your borders, in private life, and all the way up to national borders. Respect the borders of others. They are part of who and what we are. The first thing Joshua did after conquest and cleanup, was to establish borders.

chapter one hundred and eight
DO NOT DESPISE SMALL THINGS

"Cities with their Villages"

—Joshua 15:60

Note the phrase, "with their villages." Joshua attended to detail. He didn't forget little things. Many governments only care about the cities. It's quite common for country and village people to feel isolated and distant from the seat of government. But then most people even in the cities feel isolated from the government. God and His pastors look after the little people, those with no money to bribe, no influence to threaten with, no power to wield. These have the backing of God, and a good pastor should have a natural inclination towards the poor and the weak.

Note this, the Jebusites couldn't be driven out, and they dwell with the children of Judah *"...to this day"* (15:63). Many sins in the believer's life stay with them. Sanctification is a process. But in the process, we often fail to cooperate with the Holy Spirit, imagining He is robbing us of something. Sin can annoy and trouble the believer all their life. It's harder to get rid of the accusing voice of the devil reminding us of failure than it would have been to just repent in the first place. These persistent sins can distort the believer's whole personality. The devil, *"the accuser of the brethren"* (Revelation 12:10), never stops accusing God's people of their failures. He's an old nag! Never forget that God knows all about you, yet still loves you, you are His child. He is with you. He loved you while you were His enemy. He loves you more now. Never listen to the devil, never listen to his accusations. He encourages and entreats His children to *"Come to Me... take My yoke upon you and learn from Me, for I am gentle and lowly of heart, and you shall find rest for your souls*" (Matthew 11:28–29). Never give up following the Lord. Israel was still Israel despite the Jebusites.

So, what of little sins? Is there such a thing in God's eyes? Every sin nailed Jesus to the cross! After his victories, Joshua might have comfortably ignored these 'villages.' What damage could they do to Joshua or Israel? They represent a culture beyond redemption. There are many cultures that have been as bad as ancient Canaan, some modern ones much worse. The little villages presented little problems easy to deal with. Little sins are likewise. Do not integrate little sins—purge them with diligence. Make a small issue of them but deal with them. And note that there were a lot of them in these verses. A lot of small 'anything,' can make a big difference to everything! Small can be beautiful, or small can be ugly. Small can be the "*... little foxes that spoil the vines...*" (Song of Solomon 2:15).

chapter one hundred and nine

INABILITY AND REFUSAL

"And they did not drive out the Canaanites who dwelt in Gezer; but the Canaanites dwell among the Ephraimites to this day and have become forced laborers"
—Joshua 16:10

This section of Joshua continues the division of land. There are some relevant lessons here that should be of interest to leaders and Pastors. Joshua 16:10 highlights one.

Church leaders and Pastors *must be able to make distinctions between inability and refusal*. Is it a simple variation of phrase in the narrative when it says Judah *"Could not... drive out"* (15:63) and that Ephraim *"Did not... drive out"* (16:10)? There could be a world of difference between these. Perhaps one tried and failed; the other saw a business waiting to happen... they made the Canaanites "forced labour" (16: 10). Both failed, but one failure can be worse than another. Judah's heart was right. They sought to defeat their enemies. Ephraim saw that they could use their enemies for gain and forced them to serve.

These attitudes surface in the believer regarding sanctification. Joshua knew it but the people failed to obey or chose to disobey; same outcome, different attitude! The way the pastor and the church deal with people should reflect an understanding of the relevance of influences and attitudes.

Failure after genuine effort evokes empathy and help from those who observe. It doesn't change the outcome, but it modifies the experience. Not trying, or worse, using failure to further our own ends, militates against the help we need.

Both groups fail. But we all fail, don't we? We should be able to see ourselves in a brother's failure and recognize what we would have done. Lack of empathy can be a lack of self-understanding. Discipline is often more productive than help after failure. We can understand something by the repetition of failures in others.

> *Yet the children of Manasseh could not drive out the inhabitants of those cities, but the Canaanites were determined to dwell in that land. And it happened, when the children of Israel grew strong, that they put the Canaanites to forced labor, but did not utterly drive them out.*
> —Joshua 17:12–13

Here we have another tribe who "could not." They combined the failures of Judah and Ephraim. They couldn't drive them out, so they harnessed their energies for profit. The answer to sins' acceptance in the world is a church stronger in its denunciation. The church in a sinful society like ours has been given an opportunity to shine even brighter in a dark world. The answer to sin spreading through the church is extreme corporate repentance and radical change, with support for those failing.

chapter one hundred and ten
ARE YOU WHO YOU THINK YOU ARE?

Joshua 17: 14–17

> "Then the children of Joseph spoke to Joshua, saying, 'Why have you given us only one lot and one share to inherit, since we are a great people, inasmuch as the Lord has blessed us until now?'"
> —Joshua 17:14

The people weren't happy with their lot, they thought they deserved more land. Joshua's response is interesting. He firstly challenges them to act according to their declaration about themselves, "We are a great people." Yet they are afraid they will fail. Joshua confirms that they are a great people and will succeed. He says:

> You are a great people and have great power; you shall not have only one lot, but the mountain country shall be yours. Although it is wooded, you shall cut it down, and its farthest extent shall be yours; for you shall drive out the Canaanites, though they have iron chariots and are strong.
> —Joshua 17:17–18

Here Joshua is preaching. He shows the heart of a pastor. He won't let God's people slip into unbelief. Joshua believes they can take the land. If pastors don't believe that the church can win the world for Christ, what hope is there for congregations?

Joshua expects them to succeed. He expects them to trust the Lord and walk by faith, like their father Abraham, like Moses at the red sea. They, and we, are to follow in their footsteps. Believers are amazing when they are filled with faith and doing exploits for God. Too many of God's people today want heaven on earth. They have no strength or energy. We need reviving rain from heaven. Oh, that God would open the windows of heaven and pour out a blessing upon us, His church.

Preaching is supposed to enliven us to do what God has told us to do. So often we trust in education. We imagine that if the believer understands the Bible, he will live it. But we won't without the passion that affects the will into action—only applied preaching accomplishes this. The world thought education would deal with crime. It only produced educated criminals. Education just makes us intellectually fat if we aren't inspired or commanded to rise and go. Challenge is lacking in pulpits today. We have become all about information, but no action. We are like ancient Israel. Let's learn from them. Hear Joshua preach and consider your pastor. Pray for him that he will make you uncomfortable as you realize you are not what you could be for God.

The story of Joshua is heading for a close. Yet some things remain outstanding. Many would think he had done enough. Yet Joshua addressed what remained undone. How thorough is this man of God? Have you finished the work God gave you to do? Paul says to the Galatians, *"You ran well. Who hindered you from obeying the truth? This persuasion does not come from Him who calls you"* (Galatians 5:7–8). Perhaps they began to get careless, tired, without energy. This persuasion, that you don't have to obey the truth or that there is a better way, doesn't come from God. It is a lie to suggest that you can't serve or obey God—you can. Joshua believed the people could achieve their desired end if they walked by faith.

SECTION XXI:
ENTER IN!

chapter one hundred and eleven
THE SADDEST VERSE IN JOSHUA

Chapter 18

Now the whole congregation of the children of Israel assembled together at Shiloh, and set up the tabernacle of meeting there. And the land was subdued before them. But there remained among the children of Israel seven tribes which had not yet received their inheritance.

—Joshua 18:1

One of the saddest verses in the book of Joshua is here. Deep in discussions about real estate, there was a street with seven broken-down, dishevelled shacks. After all the struggles and battles, they remained without their inheritance. They had no place to call home. Not because there wasn't a place for them but because they had not "...entered in..." Feel for them, please. Everybody around was settling in, but it was like they hadn't crossed over Jordan. They might as well be in the desert in a sandstorm. Had the Israelites suffered for nothing? Many of their brethren had died so that these seven tribes could enter in. What happened? They weren't atheists or enemies, they were Israelites... living in poverty... empty when they should have been full... are you?

You don't need to be empty. You don't have to live in spiritual poverty as a believer! Jesus promised us the Holy Spirit. Jesus describes the Holy Spirit as "*Allos Paracletos*" which means "another comforter."[19]

In the Bible, there are multiple words and passages which describe the work of the Holy Spirit in the believer. Before we run to heavy linguistics, just consider WHO we are referring to—God the Holy Spirit is in the believer! No other theological or linguistic knowledge is required—God is with you. Why are you weak?!

In any gathering of God's people, there are a significant number like the Israelites, people who haven't really entered the real experience of salvation or a real walk with God. This breaks God's heart, and it breaks pastors' hearts. We read, *"But there remained among the children of Israel seven tribes which had not yet received their inheritance."* As I said, one of the saddest verses in the book of Joshua.

Joshua observed this and refused to leave them there. He rebuked them. Please note, if you aren't experiencing God like others, then it is, at one level, up to you.

Joshua told these seven tribes to get right with God and enter the land God promised them. Does this resonate in your heart as you read? If it does, cry out to the Lord. You are missing the best life you ever imagined. The world's goods can't come close to this joy.

The first thing for leaders and pastors to note is that these people are among God's people. Will you learn to recognize them? They aren't fixed on Jesus. They need a dealing with God. A gentle dealing, perhaps, or maybe a shock. The pastor's job is to address this subject strongly and kindly when it becomes visible. Today, many pastors are these people! Many pastors are lost in their ministry. They don't really know what's wrong. Listen to Joshua, you may have neglected to simply enter into your promised inheritance in Christ. Read on…

---

19 Spiros Zhodiates, New Testament: The Complete Word Study Dictionary (Iowa Falls, Iowa: Word Publishers Inc., 1992), 1107.

chapter one hundred and twelve

BEING NEGLIGENT

"Then Joshua said to the children of Israel: 'How long will you neglect to go and possess the land which the Lord God of your fathers has given you?'"
—Joshua 18:3

Joshua isn't as gentle as I have tried to be. He tells them they are guilty of "neglect." "How long will you neglect?" They saw the walls fall at Jericho. They agonized at Ai with Achan. Yet they stopped at some point, sat down and watched everybody else move on. We are not given insight into why these seven tribes neglected their inheritance. Surely to us looking on it is quite amazing! A land flowing with milk and honey. A land God promised them as a home, yet they chose poverty.

Are we like they were before Joshua's rebuke? Are we hiding on the fringes of the universal Christian church? Are we letting previous generations work while we refuse to enter into what God has planned for us? We have watched parents and grandparents struggle and sacrifice to see the gospel spread abroad. We have heard their stories of winning souls for Christ. Yet, as you read you have no spiritual struggle, no victories, no testimonies. Have you ever led someone to Jesus Christ and seen them received by Him, their lives transformed? Will there be no gems in your crown? We have left it to great names and big events and trusted in worship concerts. We expect pastors to lead sinners to Jesus, yet in a number of search committee meetings I have never been asked nor heard anybody else asked "How many souls have you led to Jesus?" We are in need of a Joshua to rebuke us towards what we were called to do: "Go up and possess the land." Joshua then gives good guidance as to where to begin.

chapter one hundred and thirteen
BEING SURVEYORS

Joshua 18: 4–10

"Pick out from among you three men for each tribe, and I will send them; they shall rise and go through the land, survey it according to their inheritance, and come back to me"

—Joshua 18:4

Here Joshua calls again on his own experience of spying out the land for Moses. He tells them to go and walk through the land. This is the charge given to every believer—a charge to experience God via His word and His Spirit. *"... desire the sincere milk of the word, that you may grow thereby"* (1 Pet 2:2).

So, Joshua charged them to go and see if Canaan was what they were told. If you are reluctant to really commit to Jesus, read the gospel again from the beginning. Check for yourself. *"...The Truth shall make you free"* (John 8:32).

Joshua adds that they "survey" the land. This is undoubtedly deeper than a 'sight-seeing.' It is a research trip that will confirm what they were told to be true or to be false. Joshua is certain that these men will return with the enthusiasm he and Caleb had when they first surveyed the land.

If you aren't prepared to examine God's promises, you are relinquishing your birthright. You have given up. You are living off the efforts of others while hiding in the shadows of your restricted life. Every believer must survey the land themselves. It will be the same conclusion— that this is a land flowing with milk and honey! It's a land worth fighting for spiritually, meant to be enjoyed and lived in to the full—the land of God's salvation. Inherit it!

"So the men went, passed through the land, and wrote the survey in a book in seven parts by cities; and they came to Joshua at the camp in Shiloh" (Joshua 18:9). So, they went, and they were so impressed that they wrote a book! A big book spread into seven parts!! What a hidden message to find in the middle of real estate! The land is big enough for all God's children. God can take you from sitting under a tree in the shade, hiding, to becoming so thrilled with the gospel you have rediscovered for yourself, that you must write it all down for posterity. These representatives of the seven tribes produced the information required for Joshua to distribute the land. Joshua did this, as the narrative tells us in the following verses, in Shiloh. Shiloh means "a place of rest"—this what you're missing if you haven't entered into your inheritance… you haven't entered into your *rest*! The seven tribes did exactly as they were told and entered into their inheritance. You can enter yours today.

chapter one hundred and fourteen
JOSHUA'S INHERITANCE

Joshua 18:11; 19:48–50

This is the historical record of the inheritance of the seven tribes. We don't need to include it here, but at the end of chapter 19 a short paragraph is given to our theme of "Being Joshua."

> *When they had made an end of dividing the land as an inheritance according to their borders, the children of Israel gave an inheritance among them to Joshua the son of Nun. According to the word of the Lord they gave him the city which he asked for, Timnath Serah in the mountains of Ephraim; and he built the city and dwelt in it.*
> —Joshua 19:49–50

Joshua led the conquest of Canaan, accompanying the tribes every step along the way—fighting with them, encouraging them, and even rebuking those who hadn't entered—spurring them on to finally receive their inheritance. Only after all of that had been accomplished does Joshua receive his inheritance. "*When they had made an end of dividing the land… the children of Israel gave an inheritance among them to Joshua the Son of Nun*" (Joshua 19: 49).

Pastors, don't expect to be first in line when God dispenses blessings. Pastors who think they are first in any way should take time out for self-examination. Rather, be content to be last and least. God often has special and unique blessings which seem to come when least expected. They are often far too big; we realize we didn't earn them. They don't satisfy our need for recognition or respect; they humble us to keep us safe from ourselves. Joshua models a standard for us after a lifetime of faithfulness. He serves everybody else, then he is served. Everybody else gets a bigger inheritance than Joshua. He chose it humbly for himself.

Now the narrative moves on to a bridging piece. The cities of refuge and the cities of the Levites. Everything is good, harmonious, pleasant, and filled with the joy of rest. But a great disturbance is about to come upon them. An insubstantial disturbance, (like many of the internal troubles of the church) resulting in a new and solidified unity. Sometimes misunderstandings are sent to cause us to reaffirm the original understanding. Baptists were known as 'radical believers' because they insisted on a return to the Bible. God also shakes things to press believers closer together... like a marriage!

chapter one hundred and fifteen
THE CITIES OF REFUGE

This is another interesting part of the biblical narrative, but not instantly related to the subject of this book. Nevertheless, I always read these scriptures. You may prefer in this instance to miss this chapter without loss to the narrative of "Being Joshua." The only point I wish to make is that there are real issues in churches. Sometimes someone must leave and go to another church. This, like these cities of refuge, may be viewed as a kind of failure. A breakdown between brethren. Pastors and churches have to live with this reality produced by our failure, or by circumstances which we seem unable to fix. It is very sad to have to leave a church because of such unusual times. But be assured the Lord understands, and in time we may return, and life goes on one way or another. That's the cities of refuge. When a church receives someone looking for similar refuge, they must extend fellowship and protection and love insofar as no sin has been committed. The church isn't perfect. Neither are its members. But while we may not be what we should be, we certainly aren't what we used to be, thank God for that. Finally, the cities of refuge weren't for petty fallouts, they were for life-threatening situations. Give serious self-examination when you want to leave the church you are presently in.

chapter one hundred and sixteen
THE PROMISE FULFILLED

So the Lord gave to Israel all the land of which He had sworn to give to their fathers, and they took possession of it and dwelt in it. The Lord gave them rest all around, according to all that He had sworn to their fathers. And not a man of all their enemies stood against them; the Lord delivered all their enemies into their hand. Not a word failed of any good thing which the Lord had spoken to the house of Israel. All came to pass.

—Joshua 21:43–45

According to most opinions, Joshua wasn't the writer of the book bearing his name. However, as you observed, he is quoted a lot. This short quote shows Joshua's character. It is thoroughly God-centred. It declares God's promises were fulfilled by Him. He tells them and us that the Lord gave them rest all around. He reminds them that not a man stood against them. Above all, in my imagination, I can hear him 'preach,' that *"Not a word failed of any good thing which the Lord had spoken to the house of Israel. All came to pass"* (21: 45). And preachers for centuries have taken his lead and preached vibrant sermons on the powerful declaratory words in this text. This is Joshua's view of the world and this period of his life. Every believer should be able to approximate his walk with God in terms like these, especially this verse just quoted.

How do you get to be like this? Well college won't do it. It requires simple, daily diligence in reading the Bible from cover to cover as often and as many times as is possible—until the Bible becomes who you are. Joshua's own words are being quoted, but they are the inspired word of God. Your words will take on the influence of the Bible, they will become a part of you. They must become who you are, or you are my dear friend… in the wrong profession. Continue this habit throughout your life, and detailed study of individual books. Once you are familiar with the whole of Scripture to a good degree, then tackle a bit of reformed theology, but be careful with theology. I have read and studied it all my life; I have also observed many lively brothers and sisters shrink in their spirituality and become cold and pharisaic, dry as dust. I have observed more to whom the great theological works became an oasis in a superficial, shallow church world. Watch for your soul. We need to know God not Calvin. (Both are good!) We need to experience Him not in mere emotional or intellectual highs. You don't have to rush this endeavour. In fact, be encouraged to take time and make it real… and keep it real!

SECTION XXII:
END TIMES BEING A MODERN PROBLEM

chapter one hundred and seventeen
THE TWO-AND-A-HALF TRIBES

The following is Israel's exhortation to enter into spiritual inheritance.

> *Then Joshua called the Reubenites, the Gadites, and half the tribe of Manasseh, and said to them: "You have kept all that Moses the servant of the Lord commanded you, and have obeyed my voice in all that I commanded you. You have not left your brethren these many days, up to this day, but have kept the charge of the commandment of the Lord your God. And now the Lord your God has given rest to your brethren, as He promised them...*
> —Joshua 22:1–4

They obeyed God and Joshua, and they didn't leave their brethren. What a testimony!

> *now therefore, return and go to your tents and to the land of your possession, which Moses the servant of the Lord gave you on the other side of the Jordan. But take careful heed to do the commandment and the law which Moses the servant of the Lord commanded you, to love the Lord your God, to walk in all His ways, to keep His commandments, to hold fast to Him, and to serve Him with all your heart and with all your soul." So Joshua blessed them and sent them away, and they went to their tents.*
> —Joshua 22:4–6

This commandment is essential—take careful heed to your soul. Love the Lord. Do His will. Hold fast to Him. That is an active faith that clings to God, His Word, and his people.

Are you listening, pastor? To serve the Lord with the heart, not just the head! This is a real danger because pastors should be theologically inclined to some degree.

> *Now to half the tribe of Manasseh Moses had given a possession in Bashan, but to the other half of it Joshua gave a possession among their brethren on this side of the Jordan, westward. And indeed, when Joshua sent them away to their tents, he blessed them, and spoke to them, saying, "Return with much riches to your tents, with very much livestock, with silver, with gold, with bronze, with iron, and with very much clothing. Divide the spoil of your enemies with your brethren."*
>
> *So the children of Reuben, the children of Gad, and half the tribe of Manasseh returned, and departed from the children of Israel at Shiloh, which is in the land of Canaan, to go to the country of Gilead, to the land of their possession, which they had obtained according to the word of the Lord by the hand of Moses.*
>
> —Joshua 22:7–9

The narrative returns in more detail to the settling of the land of Canaan because the two-and-a-half tribes discussed here didn't settle in Canaan. They settled East of Jordan. It was time for them to go home to their families. Joshua speaks kindly to them. He is totally appreciative of all that they helped accomplish and especially how they kept their word… He sends them back to their families on the other side of Jordan. The discussion is quiet and peaceable, united and grateful. It appears that a period of rest has begun. Chapter 21:43–45 is a fitting end to this long list of blessings, and it ends in verse 45 with these grand words: *"Not a word failed of any good thing which the Lord had spoken to the house of Israel. All came to pass."* Glory to God!

We could have thought the story was finished! Often however, the end of the work is interrupted, before it has had time to sigh. Read on…

chapter one hundred and eighteen
A GOSSIP IS AMONG US!

This section of the book of Joshua is essential reading. I will thread my comments through the text as you read. Italics are the Bible texts. Plain text is very clearly mine!

> *"And when they came to the region of the Jordan which is in the land of Canaan, the children of Reuben, the children of Gad, and half the tribe of Manasseh built an altar there by the Jordan—a great impressive altar"*
> —Joshua 22:10

This is a bit unexpected. Everything was fine, but nobody said anything about altars. Indeed, a "great and impressive altar." They hadn't even laid down their arms and hugged their families, but they built an altar? To what? To whom? Why? They knew, but no one else did. But word gets around. Read on...

> *Now the children of Israel heard someone say, "Behold, the children of Reuben, the children of Gad, and half the tribe of Manasseh have built an altar on the frontier of the land of Canaan, in the region of the Jordan—on the children of Israel's side"*
> —Joshua 22:11

'Heard someone say' Oh, dear! Now we have been indulging ourselves in Joshua's wisdom and leadership. I asked earlier, "Is Joshua getting tired?" Again, I am looking for something to help explain this inconsistency in an otherwise superb warrior statesman. Joshua wasn't involved here. Have you thought about what your absence will facilitate, in the church you are about to resign from? This is just a thought for which I have no hard evidence. But Joshua taking a backseat here exposes a potential weakness when a strong leader leaves the scene. It suggests the failure that his leadership was, perhaps, too singular. The Bible presents a body ministry in the New Testament. On the other hand, when you leave under the Lord's good leading, you must be ready to let it go and leave it with the Lord, whose church it is. Not as easy as it sounds.

The words and the phrases need examination. "Someone"—no name, no credibility. "Heard"—not saw! How good was their hearing? The children of Israel... heard? How did they hear? I suggest that they 'all' heard it one after the other because it was a rumour. But it was lubricated by assumptions, innuendo, and sensationalism. So, we have the accusation applied to the two-and-a-half tribes (22:11). They were singled out together as being involved in building an altar before any details were explained. The result is... like most rumours... an imaginary offence!

"And when the children of Israel heard of it, the whole congregation of the children of Israel gathered together at Shiloh to go to war against them" (Joshua 22:12).

They built an altar, and all Israel was going to go to war against them. How soon people take up arms. Weren't they tired of war? Surely there might have been a slight reluctance to fight against each other? But no. This passage is a bit Job-like. Lots of right being wrong and lots of wrong being right. Good people appearing bad and nobody reading things right.

> *Then the children of Israel sent Phinehas the son of Eleazar the priest to the children of Reuben, to the children of Gad, and to half the tribe of Manasseh, into the land of Gilead, and with him ten rulers, one ruler each from the chief house of every tribe of Israel; and each one was the head of the house of his father among the divisions of*

A Gossip is among Us!

Israel. Then they came to the children of Reuben, to the children of Gad, and to half the tribe of Manasseh, to the land of Gilead, and they spoke with them, saying...
—Joshua 22:13–15

Let's look at what they said and what happened here because these situations arise in churches regularly. Sadly, they aren't handled well. The first mistake they made was not to include their brethren in the project. They failed to see how their actions would appear from a distance... the other side of Jordan. Even Joshua seems to have failed here.

So, they came to speak, but their tone was confrontational. If the rumour is right, these tribes must be confronted. See their care for the glory of God. See their zeal for the Lord. They are fearless—but they are wrong. The two tribes did nothing wrong. Sadly, this is common in churches... 'someone said.' The members of the delegation reached for words that convey a conclusion: *"Thus says the whole congregation of the Lord: 'What treachery... that you have committed ... to turn away... from following the Lord... you have built... an altar, that you might rebel this day against the Lord?"* (Joshua 22:16). And they display their grasp of history and doctrine and the shameful failure of their fathers, but not by these men building this altar:

Is the iniquity of Peor not enough for us, from which we are not cleansed till this day, although there was a plague in the congregation of the Lord... Did not Achan the son of Zerah commit a trespass in the accursed thing, and wrath fell on all the congregation of Israel? And that man did not perish alone in his iniquity.
—Joshua 22:17, 20

They show a thorough understanding of God and His ways. Gained from their own failures! They present a very powerful case for repentance. The reply... a truly wonderful, thorough expression of fidelity to the Lord God of Israel! And they give a clear reason.

> *Then the children of Reuben, the children of Gad, and half the tribe of Manasseh answered and said to the heads of the divisions of Israel:... "... we have done it for fear, for a reason, saying, 'In time to come your descendants may speak to our descendants, saying, "What have you to do with the Lord God of Israel?"'*
> —Joshua 22:21, 24

What an awesome defence. The two-and-a-half tribes explain their motivation—devotion to the Lord and their families and progeny—because 'someone said.' Be careful what you say! Be even more careful what you do with what you hear.

Religious actions must allow examination and withstand being misread. They should have a clear explanation that relates to the scriptures. A case in point today would be the practice of worship. We should be minimizing dangers in worship, not allowing free rein of emotion. Here we have a lesson in risky expression. At least, expressions must be discussed, examined, and understood before being built.

chapter one hundred and nineteen
THE LORD IS AMONG US

The situation worked out, but it was a potential disaster. Where was Joshua? Why does he seem to be out of the picture in this serious matter? Phinehas the priest is the lead voice.

> *Now when Phinehas the priest and the rulers of the congregation, the heads of the divisions of Israel who were with him, heard the words that the children of Reuben, the children of Gad, and the children of Manasseh spoke, it pleased them. Then Phinehas the son of Eleazar the priest said to the children of Reuben, the children of Gad, and the children of Manasseh, "This day we perceive that the Lord is among us..."*
> —Joshua 22:30–31

The conclusion of the matter is awesome! God give us conclusions to division like this more often! We should ask ourselves regularly, "Is the Lord among us?" We should have parameters and people who can assess this. We should be looking for the Lord among us every time we meet, yes, every time! Otherwise, we are just a mutual-aid society. The evidence here was the diligence to fight for God's honour. This illustrated a well-defined spiritual reason behind the action. The mutual statements of acceptance and unity produced fellowship in the nation bringing a satisfying resolution at the end of the day.

"*This day we perceive that the Lord is among us.*" What an end to a difficult day. Make it your daily aim to 'perceive that the

Lord is with you.' Whoever you are with, bring the Lord into that moment—make it a perceptible experience. Become sensitive to His presence, and more conscious when it is absent! Talk about Jesus and His love. Pastors, do you have meetings that are more than practicality. How often is the meeting a time of absolute fullness of God's Spirit that silences 'guy-talk?' *Do our elders' meetings "... perceive that the Lord is among us?"* Consider how often this is the case in our Christian walk... you will be surprised to realize that He is with you, among you, more often than you realize.

Although Joshua wasn't there, the skills of his people are encouraging. Joshua has led them well. His influences are among all the tribes and their leaders. He can, perhaps, rest for a while knowing that Phinehas will handle it well. Phinehas does, and please note that he was fully prepared to do battle or make peace. This is Joshua's administration. This is the mature long-term effect of Joshua the statesman. God give us elders like these men. God give us seniors like Joshua. God give us men, women, youth, and children like this; Lord, make me like Joshua!

SECTION XXIII: CHOOSE TODAY

chapter one hundred and twenty

JOSHUA'S FAREWELL ADDRESS

These last two chapters are about Joshua, Israel, and the Lord, similar in tone to the first chapter. A long time has passed since the incident of the 'great and impressive altar.'

"*Now it came to pass, a long time after the Lord had given rest to Israel from all their enemies round about, that Joshua was old, advanced in age*" (Joshua 23:1). Old age doesn't come on its own. We hope it comes with health, family, and security. We only have these things if we prepare before it comes. Better to start when you're twenty rather than wait. Above all, learn in life to be content with what you have. Learn, in whatever circumstances, to say like Paul:

> *for I have learned in whatever state I am, to be content: I know how to be abased, and I know how to abound. Everywhere and in all things I have learned both to be full and to be hungry, both to abound and to suffer need. I can do all things through Christ who strengthens me.*
> —Phil. 4:11–13

When you reach old age, you will be the man you are. It is hard to hide him, to fake him. So, work on him, improve him. One thing to try to grasp is how quickly old age arrives… earlier for some, later for others, but always too soon. I have sat at hospital beds and heard men well into their eighties say, "I hoped I would have lived a bit longer." Generally, not because they enjoyed age, but they enjoyed their grandchildren! Growing old is a privilege, to be enjoyed as you loosen your grip on the many good things in this world.

Being Joshua

A long time passed after Joshua stopped campaigning. He now had rest. It can be difficult to stop when you retire. It's a whole new life, full of fresh challenges, different opportunities. Joshua lived it. He was "old and advanced in age." But he still had something to say.

> *And Joshua called for all Israel, for their elders, for their heads, for their judges, and for their officers, and said to them: "I am old, advanced in age. You have seen all that the Lord your God has done to all these nations because of you, for the Lord your God is He who has fought for you.*
> —Joshua 23:2–3

He isn't just talking about himself. He talks about what they had witnessed the Lord do. One sentence is what Joshua says about himself: *"See, I have divided to you by lot these nations that remain, to be an inheritance for your tribes, from the Jordan, with all the nations that I have cut off, as far as the Great Sea westward"* (Joshua 23:4).

What a man! Joshua—a man to emulate, study, and learn from.

chapter one hundred and twenty-one

THE WORD OF GOD BEING FRONT AND CENTRE

And the Lord your God will expel them from before you and drive them out of your sight. So you shall possess their land, as the Lord your God promised you. Therefore be very courageous to keep and to do all that is written in the Book of the Law of Moses, lest you turn aside from it to the right hand or to the left, and lest you go among these nations, these who remain among you...

—Joshua 23:5–7

Joshua encouraged them to be courageous and believe that God keeps His promises. He assures them they will possess the land that remains. He lays upon them a spiritual charge: *"To keep and to do all that is written in the Book of the Law."* God's Word is never to be a background thing in our lives. It must never be secondary or relegated to a shelf. It must be front and centre, part of our conversations, and constantly on our hearts and minds, especially if... we would be a Joshua.

Hear the echo of the conversation God had with Joshua in the first chapter: "be very courageous." Joshua is over one hundred years old. These words which he heard when he was eighty years old are as fresh as ever. You can feel the energy and exhilaration he feels as he speaks. This energy isn't just a love for life. He is speaking about a living, vibrant relationship with the almighty God. He knows this walk with God so well. In his old age, it hadn't diminished. He gives sundry admonitions to keep the word of God and be faithful to Him. Summed up, Joshua tells them that if they hold to these principles and precepts, they will succeed. They will not just succeed as a nation, but the nation will succeed because: *"One man of you shall chase a thousand..."* (Joshua 23:10). Never allow the devil or anyone else to tell you that you are not important to God and His work. Remember that which Joshua argues here—one man can do extraordinary feats for God.

See Joshua's attention to detail, all of it requiring a constant, conscious dedication. *"You shall not make mention of the names of their gods..."* How easy with time to lay aside strictures, to ease back and become moderate, to satisfy the desire to be nice. Including God in your life has implications that require diligent application. But it isn't servitude or rigour. These were left behind in Egypt. Joshua exhorts Israel not to be careless about the gods of the world. These we should actively shun. Beware of worldliness, it's a chameleon. Reject it with energy. Refuse it with determination. Ask yourself "What is worldliness today in its practical expression?" If you ask around, the definitions are increasingly vague, suggesting we don't know—worldliness isn't feared anymore. It is a difficult yet essential topic for pastors to address, though doing so won't make them popular. Joshua called attention to the danger. If you never warn your congregation or Christian friends, as he did, do you really care for their souls?

> *Behold, this day I am going the way of all the earth. And you know in all your hearts and in all your souls that not one thing has failed of all the good things which the Lord your God spoke concerning you. All have come to pass for you; not one word of them has failed.*
> —Joshua 23:14

What an awesome thing to be able to say at the end of your life. It should be our testimony.

Joshua's closing statement reminds us of the blessings and curses of Mount Gerizim and Mount Ebal. There Moses laid out before Israel two paths. On Mount Gerizim, a life of obedience which would be filled with blessing, and on Mount Ebal, a life of disobedience and curses (Deut. 11:26–29). Joshua reminded Israel of their history. These words were to warn, not condemn. Make sure you heed the warnings!

SECTION XXIV:
LAST WORDS

chapter one hundred and twenty-two
LAST WORDS BEING IMPRESSIVE

Joshua 24

The Covenant at Shechem.
This is another detailed reading but so inspiring it must be read. For Joshua, his relationship with God wasn't just a phase of his young life or a moment of valour in his mid-years. It was a lifelong vibrant personal relationship with God. Things he relates from days long gone sound as fresh as when they happened. You can feel this as you read. God give us old men with such conviction and experience. Men that inspire us to devotion in Christ and His cause. Aim to be such a man before you become a pastor. In this last chapter, Joshua will speak prophetically as if God was the speaker. Oh, please God give us pastors who can speak thus at least from time to time, that their words might carry the authenticity of Joshua's in his closing address.

> *Then Joshua gathered all the tribes of Israel to Shechem and called for the elders of Israel, for their heads, for their judges, and for their officers; and they presented themselves before God. And Joshua said to all the people, "Thus says the Lord God of Israel: 'Your fathers, including Terah, the father of Abraham and the father of Nahor, dwelt on the other side of the River in old times; and they served other gods. Then I took your father Abraham from the other side of the River, led him throughout all the land of Canaan, and multiplied his descendants and gave him*

Being Joshua

Isaac. To Isaac I gave Jacob and Esau. To Esau I gave the mountains of Seir to possess, but Jacob and his children went down to Egypt. Also I sent Moses and Aaron, and I plagued Egypt, according to what I did among them. Afterward I brought you out.

'Then I brought your fathers out of Egypt, and you came to the sea; and the Egyptians pursued your fathers with chariots and horsemen to the Red Sea. So they cried out to the Lord; and He put darkness between you and the Egyptians, brought the sea upon them, and covered them. And your eyes saw what I did in Egypt. Then you dwelt in the wilderness a long time. And I brought you into the land of the Amorites, who dwelt on the other side of the Jordan, and they fought with you. But I gave them into your hand, that you might possess their land, and I destroyed them from before you. Then Balak the son of Zippor, king of Moab, arose to make war against Israel, and sent and called Balaam the son of Beor to curse you. But I would not listen to Balaam; therefore he continued to bless you. So I delivered you out of his hand. Then you went over the Jordan and came to Jericho. And the men of Jericho fought against you—also the Amorites, the Perizzites, the Canaanites, the Hittites, the Girgashites, the Hivites, and the Jebusites. But I delivered them into your hand. I sent the hornet before you which drove them out from before you, also the two kings of the Amorites, but not with your sword or with your bow. I have given you a land for which you did not labor, and cities which you did not build, and you dwell in them; you eat of the vineyards and olive groves which you did not plant.'

—Joshua 24:1–13

chapter one hundred and twenty-three

PREACH IT, BROTHER!

Now therefore, fear the Lord, serve Him in sincerity and in truth, and put away the gods which your fathers served on the other side of the River and in Egypt. Serve the Lord! And if it seems evil to you to serve the Lord, choose for yourselves this day whom you will serve, whether the gods which your fathers served that were on the other side of the River, or the gods of the Amorites, in whose land you dwell. But as for me and my house, we will serve the Lord.
—Joshua 24:14–15

These words are among the most inspiring words in the book of Joshua, among the most powerful in the Bible. Delivered by an old man, from a heart in touch with God over a long period of time. Joshua is still addressing you and I in the 21st century with these same words. They are still pertinently relevant: "... *choose for yourselves this day whom you will serve... But as for me and my house we will serve the Lord*" (24:15).

Joshua understood people. He wasn't afraid to address them in easy-to-understand terms. Today, his manner would be unacceptable because we are more interested in the method of delivery than the content! Those of us too old to be poisoned by this foolishness know that the only reason Joshua is speaking at all is due to his life of affection and service to the nation. He loved them. But the real world lay before them with threatening temptations. This wasn't a time to care about a difficult choice of words. The concern now was clarity and effective communication to result in understanding and actions that would last a lifetime. Nice feelings are such a trifling irrelevance in life's serious moments, Every Sunday sermon is a serious moment, potentially life-changing!

The Israelites received this word from God and responded with assured compliance. If you want to depress the preacher, say to him, as was once said to me in a church in Scotland, "Thank you Reverend, your sermon was very nice!" Say nothing to the preacher, he isn't looking for compliments, let alone complaints. Just go home and get right with God! The nation wanted to respond to Joshua out of gratitude. Their words weren't about Joshua but the Lord's dealings with them. Now that's a successful sermon; that's a successful life.

The people echo Joshua's reading of history as a reason for obedience: "... *far be it from us that we should forsake the Lord to serve other gods...*" (Joshua 24:16). For most of us, this would be the end of the conversation. A little worship time and a cuppa and off home to watch sports on TV. Not Joshua! Unmoved, he says, "*You can't serve the Lord...*" (24:19)! Can you believe this?! Just when we think things are winding down... perhaps we don't need to read anymore... it's just a doxology... Then, in the closing verses of the Book of Joshua, God is still speaking through him. We really should read on.

> *But Joshua said to the people, "You cannot serve the Lord, for He is a holy God. He is a jealous God; He will not forgive your transgressions nor your sins. If you forsake the Lord and serve foreign gods, then He will turn and do you harm and consume you, after He has done you good."*
> —Joshua 24:19–20

How would you feel if the pastor met your appreciation for his sermon saying, "Yes but you will not obey the Lord!" Oh, I can hear the elders firing you before lunch! These people had a stronger spiritual constitution than us—and we are the New Testament church! They were fighters! Verse 21 says, "*And the people said to Joshua, 'No, but we will serve the Lord!'*"

Israel isn't easy to offend. Neither should a pastor be! They coped with strong words. They stood their ground and affirmed their intention: *"No, but we will serve the Lord!"* Surely Joshua would compliment them now... absolutely not...! *"So Joshua said to the people, 'You are witnesses against yourselves that you have chosen the Lord for yourselves, to serve Him'"* (Joshua 24:22).

Joshua turned their words on them: "*You are witnesses against yourselves...*" Yet again they are unoffended. This is a serious exchange. This is a real sermon. It is demanding. It looks for a life commitment...as every sermon should! Why do we settle for less than a full commitment from a congregation who boldly declare they are present to hear and to obey? Why the brevity? Why the carefulness and fear? Israel responded, meeting Joshua's accusations head-on. They said, "*We are witnesses!*" And witnesses they were. And witnesses we are too. Make sure your life is a witness to your faithfulness to God.

When did you last hear a sermon that induced such a conversation with a congregation? This used to be the norm. This is the method that produced the church. Joshua wasn't content with them repeating his words or with their obedient intentions.... He wanted to see evidence! Preacher, pastor, elders, leaders, this is good biblical preaching. This isn't college homiletics or apologetics. This is biblical preaching. The church needs a new generation of preachers like Joshua. Joshua attacks the sleepy church like he attacked the five kings. Like many an old preacher, he stayed up preparing all night and shocks them before they were properly awake! Joshua wanted physical evidence.

> *"Now therefore,"* he said, *"put away the foreign gods which are among you, and incline your heart to the Lord God of Israel."* And the people said to Joshua, *"The Lord our God we will serve, and His voice we will obey!"*
>
> *So Joshua made a covenant with the people that day, and made for them a statute and an ordinance in Shechem. Then Joshua wrote these words in the book of the Law of*

> *God. And he took a large stone, and set it up there under the oak that was by the sanctuary of the Lord. And Joshua said to all the people, "Behold, this stone shall be a witness to us, for it has heard all the words of the Lord which He spoke to us. It shall therefore be a witness to you, lest you deny your God." So Joshua let the people depart, each to his own inheritance.*
>
> —Joshua 24:23–28

Joshua didn't stop after hearing their verbal assurances. He demanded a covenant in writing. And still, Israel honoured Joshua and made a covenant. Joshua wrote it down for posterity, for us to judge. Oh, God make us preachers like Joshua. Men who clearly delineate the reality of sinners before a holy God. Demand, in God's name, a response, and get it. Drive it home and make it memorable. Our land would be healed in a year. The following verses tell us the effect resulting from such sermons based upon the word of God. What happened after the sermon was over? What happened when the people got home to their inheritance? How about the middle of the week? Did they still remember the sermon? They certainly did.

Joshua would soon die and be buried. Like all of us soon after, he would recede from the consciousness of his congregation. But life goes on. Did they live according to their protestation? Read these last verses in the book of Joshua. If you have any ambition to be a 'Joshua,' recognize what you must become and what fruit you will have for your labours if you do.

chapter one hundred and twenty-four
THE DEATH OF JOSHUA AND ELEAZAR

Now it came to pass after these things that Joshua the son of Nun, the servant of the Lord, died, being one hundred and ten years old. And they buried him within the border of his inheritance at Timnath Serah, which is in the mountains of Ephraim, on the north side of Mount Gaash.

Israel served the Lord all the days of Joshua, and all the days of the elders who outlived Joshua, who had known all the works of the Lord which He had done for Israel.

—Joshua 24:29–31

Joshua 24:31 tells us Israel served the Lord all the days of Joshua and all the days of the elders who outlived Joshua. That is a testimony to this man, his methods, and his God. And hear this dear reader: Jericho remained 'shut up' all the days of Joshua and until this day! That's what serving God can accomplish.

CONCLUSION

The bones of Joseph, which the children of Israel had brought up out of Egypt, they buried at Shechem, in the plot of ground which Jacob had bought from the sons of Hamor the father of Shechem for one hundred pieces of silver, and which had become an inheritance of the children of Joseph.

—Joshua 24:32

This verse isn't directly about Joshua. I include it to show that the Bible presents the connection between these great men of faith. Joseph took them down to Egypt. Joshua brought them into the Promised Land, and the great man Moses stood between them with outstretched arms spanning the centuries. We are also included in that group of men. We are all one in Christ Jesus with all the saints throughout history.

Dear reader, would you be a servant of God? We must see ourselves pertinently in this line of heroes. We must rise to the challenge and become what we presently are not. We must aspire to do great things for God. Without a doubt, we live in the last days. So, what should we do…?

do this, knowing the time, that now it is high time to awake out of sleep; for now our salvation is nearer than when we first believed. The night is far spent, the day is at hand. Therefore let us cast off the works of darkness, and let us put on the armor of light. Let us walk properly, as in the day, not in revelry and drunkenness, not in lewdness and lust, not in strife and envy. But put on the Lord Jesus Christ, and make no provision for the flesh, to fulfill its lusts.

—Romans 13:11–14

THE END

ABOUT THE AUTHOR

I became a believer when I was thirteen. At seventeen, I felt a clear call to the Christian ministry. It came when I read this verse written by Paul: *"the hearts of the saints have been refreshed by you"* (Philemon 1:7). That notion of refreshing God's people by His Holy Word came to me as a clear call to the Christian ministry. That call and that passion have never left me to this day.

I had so many doubts and fears regarding the awesome responsibility and my own fitness that I didn't go into the ministry until I was forty-four. By that time I had worked for years in the engineering industry, the pharmaceutical industry, and business, where I learned about myself, life, and men as they are. I was concurrently a highly committed member of two wonderful Bible-believing churches. There I learned about the things of God and God's people as they are!

Eventually, and only after the persistent pressure of friends and the Holy Spirit and a further seven years of university, I was ordained a minister of the gospel in a Baptist church in Scotland, where I served for twelve years. I then received a call to a church in Ontario, Canada, where I served for thirteen years. My passion throughout life, and especially during my twenty-five years in pastoral ministry, has been to teach the Scriptures, to "let the Bible speak," and to share the gospel of Jesus Christ at every opportunity. At this point in life I hope to continue in that calling and perhaps, humbly, share the Word of God with a wider audience via writing.

When wee David, faced with Goliath, took up his sling, he said, *"Is there not a cause?"* (1 Samuel 17:29). As I take up my pen, dear reader, I say to you, Are there not still giants hurling insults at God's people? Are God's people not frequently abused, misrepresented, hated without cause, sold into slavery, and alone? Today there is a need for the church to be the salt of the earth. To be a light in the world. To rise up and be heard. To rise out of oppression, speak the word loudly and powerfully, and back it by unashamed Godly living. Joshua is a wonderful example to learn from.

I have been married to Helen, a nurse, for forty-nine years. We have four adult children and three grandchildren. I have many interests, including old cars, music (acoustic and bass guitar), archery, photography, and watercolour painting. I'm a Scotsman who left Scotland, the "Land of the Bible" (as it was known in better bygone days). I came to Canada, this land of milk and honey, in 2003 to serve a church as interim pastor for six months. God had different plans! The church called me to be their senior pastor, and I accepted. My family joined me in 2004, and we served the Lord there for thirteen years. In 2016 we received the priceless gift of citizenship in Canada. Somewhat ironically, to achieve Canadian citizenship we had to swear allegiance to the queen of England! God has a sense of humour and knows how to keep a Scotsman humble!

Thank you for reading my book. I would love to hear for you, send me an email, the Lord bless you and give you peace in Jesus.

Rev. Archie Murray, August 2021
Lobo, Southern Ontario, Canada

        Email: archiemurray7@gmail.com
        Instagram: ArchieMurray10
        YouTube: Archie's Cabin

Also by the Author

Being Joseph

ISBN: 978-1-4866-1573-5

Have you ever felt betrayed by a family member? Have you ever needed even a glimpse of hope to help you through a tough situation? In the Old Testament, we read that Joseph was thrown into a pit and then sold by his own brothers. This great betrayal left him feeling alone and in despair. Unfortunately, this was only the beginning of his troubles.

Being Joseph takes a closer, pastoral perspective on perseverance through hardships, the value of forgiveness even when it's near impossible, and the redemptive hope of reconciliation. Joseph's story expands on dreams, slavery, seduction, imprisonment, and the restoration of a family. In the worst moments of Joseph's life, we can see that God never left his side. The lessons we can learn from this book can help enrich our daily lives in this difficult world today.

All ages will benefit from this captivating commentary on a real family, just like yours.

Also by the Author

Being Ruth

ISBN: 978-1-4866-1709-8

Have you ever felt like your faith was being tested? Have you ever experienced the death of a loved one? The book of Ruth, found in the Old Testament, is a moving story of a sad tragedy followed by an unrelenting commitment, both human and divine. Ruth's sadness is followed by hope deferred, yet undeterred.

Being Ruth takes a closer pastoral perspective on the shape of human expressions and relationships, the significance of names, and the consequences of men dying childless. We see Ruth, the committed daughter-in-law to Naomi, responding with grace during a difficult time in life. Although this is not your typical love story, as you allow the Scriptures to speak you'll find a beautifully enchanting story.

www.ingramcontent.com/pod-product-compliance
Lightning Source LLC
Chambersburg PA
CBHW030603230426
43661CB00053B/1826